SPEAKING ILL OF THE DEAD:

Jerks in Boston History

SPEAKING ILL OF THE DEAD:

Jerks in Boston History

Paul Della Valle

Guilford, Connecticut

Text design by Sheryl P. Kober
Project editor: Lauren Szalkiewicz
Layout artist: Justin Marciano

Library of Congress Cataloging-in-Publication Data

Della Valle, Paul.
  Speaking ill of the dead : jerks in Boston history / Paul Della Valle.
    pages cm
  Summary: "The lives of notorious bad guys, perpetrators of mischief,
visionary-if misunderstood-thinkers, and other colorful antiheroes,
jerks, and evil doers from history all get their due in the short
essays featured in these enlightening, informative, books. Speaking Ill
of the Dead: Jerks in Boston History features eighteen short
biographies of nefarious characters, from the pompous and
self-righteous Cotton Mather to the swindler Charles Ponzi"— Provided
by publisher.
  ISBN 978-0-7627-7915-4 (pbk.)
  1. Boston (Mass.)—History—Anecdotes. 2. Boston
(Mass.)—Biography—Anecdotes. 3.
Outlaws—Massachusetts—Boston—Biography—Anecdotes. 4. Rogues and
vagabonds—Massachusetts—Boston—Biography—Anecdotes. 5.
Criminals—Massachusetts—Boston—Biography—Anecdotes. I. Title. II.
Title: Jerks in Boston history.
  F73.36.D45 2013
  974.4'61—dc23

                                                              2013019040

Printed in the United States of America

10 9 8 7 6 5 4 3 2 1

To Karen: my wife, my best friend, and my muse

Contents

CONTENTS

Introduction

Who is a jerk?

In 2009 Globe Pequot Press published my book *Massachusetts Troublemakers: Rebels, Reformers, and Radicals from the Bay State*. The book was about contrarians from my home state and included Samuel Adams, Henry David Thoreau, Dorothea Dix, and Lucy Stone. All twenty essays were about people who went against the grain of society—Stone, for example, was an abolitionist when abolitionists were reviled in many places, even in the North, and she was an early feminist who had eggs and rocks thrown at her when she spoke on women's rights.

I was moved by my troublemakers' tragedies and by their commitment to causes. Dix gave her entire adult life to better the treatment of the insane and Adams sacrificed everything to further the cause of liberty—his neighbors even had to chip in to buy him a suit of clothes to wear to the Continental Congress. So many of my troublemakers persevered, despite overwhelming hardships and heartbreak. Adams saw four of his five children die before him, and Boston's Mayor of the Poor, James Michael Curley, outlived seven of his nine children.

When Globe Pequot asked me to write *Speaking Ill of the Dead: Jerks in Boston History,* I thought perhaps I would not be so moved by my subjects. After all, they would be jerks, right? I knew Curley would be in this book too, because many in Boston still consider him a jerk, although my Grandpa from County Tipperary, my Nana from Southie, and most Irish immigrants considered him a saint. But my other jerks, I figured, would get no sympathy from me.

Boy, was I wrong. Even jerks are people and once again my research helped me to see their humanity. Cotton Mather was a pompous and self-righteous arse, but he buried thirteen of his fifteen children and the pain his incorrigible son caused him evokes sympathy even four centuries later. Serial killer Jane Toppan, like most serial killers, was terribly abused and had a horrible childhood, as did Albert DeSalvo, the Boston Strangler, who watched his alcoholic father break his mother's fingers one by one. Thomas Hutchinson, the last royal governor, remains one of the most reviled men in Boston history, but his love of his family and of this place would soften any heart. Pretentious Bronson Alcott was indeed, as Thomas Carlyle noted, "a bottomless imbecile," and lazy. He let his wife and daughters do all the hard physical work at Fruitlands while he yapped and opined. But his family loved him, and, even today, when I'm in my classroom at Clinton High School, I try to employ much of the child-centered educational philosophy he championed almost two hundred years ago.

A few of the jerks I found had no redeeming qualities—Benjamin Church, for example, was a duplicitous spy who would have traded his young country's freedom for a handful of dollars during the Revolution; and Charles Stuart, who murdered his pregnant wife and blamed a black man, was so cunning in his treachery that even mental health experts found him abhorrent.

I felt bad for some of my jerk's spouses and children, especially for Rose Ponzi. Not only was she married to a jerk, the swindler Charles Ponzi, who abandoned her, but she later worked for Barney Welansky, the jerk who owned the Cocoanut Grove nightclub and ignored fire safety regulations, costing almost five hundred people their lives.

With most of the jerks, my research revealed some decency, or at least some reason they turned out the way they did. Even Ponzi, the schemer, once painfully donated patches of his own skin to be grafted on a burn victim. The great novelist John Updike once said it is hard to dislike any man once you have played a round of golf with him. So too, when you research jerks. We are all human; we all have our frailties and demons; and even jerks have some small amount of good, or at least some humanness, in them.

Doing the research for this book was a lot of work, a lot of fun, and enlightening. The cliché is to "write what you know," but writing a book like this is more about discovery. For example, I knew through family and neighborhood stories I heard while growing up in Quincy and Weymouth that my grandfathers faced prejudice when they arrived in Boston—one from Abruzzi, Italy, in the 1920s and the other, as I mentioned, from Tipperary, Ireland, a decade earlier. I never realized, however, until I researched *Massachusetts Troublemakers* and this book just how institutionalized that bias was, or how far we have come. Boston's history is marked by intolerance—blue-blooded Henry Cabot Lodge would have considered my grandfathers from "inferior stock" and many chapters in this book are colored by that kind of prejudice. It started with the Puritans, who pretty much hated everyone else. Their heirs, the Boston Brahmins, hated the Jews and Irish and Italians, and anyone who was Catholic. They especially feared anything even vaguely sexual, giving rise to the phrase "Banned in Boston." (I can just picture thought-cop J. Franklin Chase, subject of one chapter, spinning like a top in his grave whenever gays kiss after they say "I do" in Massachusetts.) Basically all the white ethnic groups, but especially the Irish, discriminated against blacks—as late as the 1950s, Boston Celtics great Bill Russell called the Hub "a flea market of racism."

But you know what? Now we have a black governor and Boston has an Italian mayor. We have gay weddings. Our favorite son, John Fitzgerald Kennedy, was the first Catholic ever elected president. Sometimes it has been painful, sometimes the jerks did seize control, but Boston has moved inexorably forward to truly become "The City on the Hill," a shining and progressive example for the rest of the country.

This book is about eighteen of the biggest jerks in Boston's history, but for every jerk I read about while I researched, I found a dozen good people—the heroes of the Cocoanut Grove fire and the Great Boston Molasses Disaster; the *Boston Post* reporters who won a Pulitzer Prize for bringing the scheme of Charles Ponzi to light; the courageous Paul Revere; and Robert Calef, who risked lawsuits and prison by publicly calling out Cotton Mather for being the fraud and jerk that he was.

Writing this book reminded me again how much I love this city and state and how proud I am to be a Bostonian, even when the Patriots blow the Super Bowl and the Sox do wicked bad.

I would be a total jerk if I did not acknowledge some of the people who have made writing this book possible. They include my editors Erin Turner, Courtney Oppel, and Lauren Szalkiewicz, who graciously helped me with advice and patience, layout artist Justin Marciano and copyeditor Grace Jeromski, and all the other folks at Globe Pequot. They include my son Rocky and my daughters Lisa and Jewel, and my daughter-in-law Michelle, my step-kids Rory and Devin, and especially my grandchildren Lucy and Reed, because when I am indulging myself with research and writing I am not hanging out with them (or mowing the lawn or cutting firewood). They include my golfing buddies, particularly in the Berlin Twilight League, who every Tuesday afternoon have to listen to tales about jerks as we hack around nine holes. They include my colleagues and my students at Clinton High who also get bombarded with jerk trivia. Finally, my wife Karen Sharpe. She could have married someone who made a lot of money. Instead she got stuck with a man who likes to write and who likes to teach kids how to write, and who, truth be told, can be a total jerk on occasion.

CHAPTER I

Cotton Mather
"A very great liar"

Cotton Mather had a lot of things going for him, but bottom line, he was a jerk.

It is not just because of his foofy glam-rock hairdo, pompous first name, his use of capiTal Letters for no reason, and atrocious spelling, but also his self-righteousness, his Puritan bias of racial superiority, and his fixation on witches.

Did we mention that, like his dear old dad Increase Mather, Cotton was also a bit of a pedophile/pervert?

"The diary of Cotton Mather is a treasure-trove to the abnormal psychologist," historian Marion Starkey wrote in her essay "The Devil and Cotton Mather," published in *Puritanism in Early America,* in 1950. "What a crooked and diseased mind lay back of those eyes that were forever spying out occasions to magnify self!"

Cotton Mather has been seen as a jerk for a long time—including in his own time when he and his father were publicly accused of feeling up a seventeen-year-old girl who was supposedly possessed. A nineteenth-century biographer who wrote favorably about Mather acknowledged he did not have a great reputation.

"I shall doubtless expose myself to little less than the contempt of many serious students of Colonial history," wrote Barrett Wendell in 1891 in the introduction to his *Cotton Mather: The Puritan Priest.* "The man's veracity has been seriously questioned; and one can see why . . . having a ready tongue and pen, he gave utterance to many hasty things not always consistent with fact or with each other. Wherefore such of posterity as have not loved his memory have inclined now and again to call him by a name he would probably have been the first to use in their place—a very great liar."

Cotton and Increase, and Cotton's grandfathers Richard Mather and John Cotton, are still celebrated as the ultimate Puritan

Cottonus Matherus
S. Theologiæ Doctor Regiæ Societatis Londinensis Socius,
et Ecclesiæ apud Bostonum Nov-Anglorum nuper Præpositus.
Ætatis Suæ LXV. MDCCXXVII.   P.Pelham ad vivum pinxit et Græce fecit et excud.

Cotton Mather

clergymen, and as founders and spiritual leaders of the Massachusetts Bay Colony, based in seventeenth-century Boston. Undoubtedly they were spiritual leaders to the Puritans, but that was a pretty small segment of humankind even then. The Puritans hated the French, Quakers, and Catholics, and they thought the Native Americans—whose land they had no qualms about stealing—less than human and cheered for their extinction.

Schoolchildren are often taught that the Puritans came to America for religious freedom. The only problem with that is the Puritans did not actually believe in religious freedom. They wanted their freedom to be Puritans, but in early Boston that was all you could be. When Roger Williams, the founder of Rhode Island, questioned why people could be publicly whipped for fishing on Sundays, and why supposedly good Christians could steal the natives' land, he was denounced by none other than Mather's granddaddy John Cotton and driven out of the Massachusetts Bay Colony by Governor John Winthrop.

To be fair, history tells us that Cotton Mather had some good qualities. Of course, history is written by the winners, and the Puritans were clearly the winners in seventeenth-century New England. Cotton's affability and earnestness, made Mather—as Kenneth Silverman, author of *The Life and Times of Cotton Mather,* observed—"the most noted conversationalist of his time, much admired and sought after by contemporaries for his erudite and beguiling wit."

An amateur scientist, Mather championed inoculations that could stem smallpox epidemics even when others thought inoculations were quackery. He knew sorrow—Mather outlived thirteen of his fifteen kids and two of his wives. His third wife was, according to Mather himself, certifiably crazy. His son Increase, named after Cotton's dad, caused him immense sorrow. Feeling bad for Cotton Mather is OK, except that on the two greatest matters of his time, he was self-righteously wrong.

Writing years after King Philip's War in 1676–1677 had basically ended the Native American presence in Massachusetts, Cotton described the 1616–1618 plague and three subsequent plagues brought to America by Europeans that had decimated the New England tribes as blessings from God.

"The woods were almost cleared of those pernicious creatures, to make room for a better growth," he wrote. Cotton and his father, and many other Puritans, believed the Nipmuc, Wampanoag, Narragansett, and other tribes that lived in seventeenth-century New England were the children of the devil. Neither Mather ever changed that view.

"Though we know not when or how these Indians first became inhabitants of this mighty continent, yet we may guess that probably the Devil decoyed those miserable savages hither in hopes that the gospel of the Lord Jesus Christ would never come here to destroy or disturb his absolute empire over them," Cotton wrote in his opus *Magnalia Christi Americana* in 1702.

Although they disagreed on some points, both Mathers played big roles in the Salem Witch trials. In 1692 when nineteen people convicted of witchcraft were hanged there—and a twentieth was crushed between stones—Cotton was one of the main voices calling for their persecution.

"It has been said, [Cotton Mather] was simultaneously the most intelligent and the most stupid man this country has ever produced," according to Carl Sifakis, author of *The Encyclopedia of American Crime*. "He was the author of no less than 450 books on many erudite subjects, but he was also obsessed by witches. With his fiery sermons, Mather was probably the man most responsible for the Salem witchcraft mania of 1692. . . . Among the many contributions Dr. Mather made on the general subject of witchcraft was the theory that the devil spoke perfect Greek, Hebrew and Latin, but that his English was hampered by an odd accent."

Cotton Mather was born in 1663 in Boston, son of Increase and Maria Mather. His path was clear from the start. Not only was his father an influential Puritan minister, but his paternal grandfather, Richard Mather, was also. His maternal grandfather, John Cotton, was the most important preacher in the first generation of Puritans who settled Boston in the 1630s. Anne Hutchinson, who, like Williams was later exiled from Massachusetts Bay Colony for disagreeing with the church/government authorities, originally came to Boston because she followed John Cotton there.

Cotton Mather entered Harvard College at twelve years old, just like dear old dad had done, and he graduated in 1678. He earned his master's degree from Harvard three years later, but by 1680 he was already preaching in churches in Dorchester and Boston. He overcame a stutter by speaking deliberately, a style that marked his sermons throughout the rest of his life.

"It was during this time that one of his old schoolmasters, Elijah Corlet, came to visit," according to author Norma Jean Lutz. "Perhaps this elderly man understood Mather's desire to preach. At any rate, he instructed Mather to compare his speaking with singing, "for as in singing there is no one who stammers, so by prolonging your pronunciation you will get a habit of speaking without hesitation."

Mather, using his more deliberate speech pattern, preached his first sermon in what had once been Richard Mather's church in Dorchester. The next week he preached in his father's house of worship, Second Church (later called the Old North Church) in Boston. He also preached in the Boston church where John Cotton had once preached. His sermons were well received and church members at the Old North Church urged Increase to make Cotton his colleague. Increase Mather resisted, but finally, after five years, Increase agreed and Cotton was ordained in North Church on May 13, 1685. He served with his father at the church until Increase died almost forty years later.

Cotton Mather married Abigail Phillips in 1686. The couple had nine children before she died in 1702. Cotton then married a widow, Elizabeth Hubbard, with whom he had six more children. The end of their happiness came quickly. On November 1, 1713, Elizabeth gave birth to twins. They named the girl Martha and the boy Eleazer. A few days later, Elizabeth and their two-year-old daughter, Jerusha, came down with the measles. First Elizabeth died, then both the infant twins, and finally Jerusha. "My lovely Jerusha expires," Mather wrote. "She was Two years, and about Seven Months old. . . . Lord, I am oppressed; undertake for me."

Mather married another widow, Lydia Lee George, in 1715. By then, nine of his fifteen children from his previous marriages had died. Four more would die before he passed away in 1728. His thirteen-year marriage to Lydia was not a happy one. He might have been a jerk, but she was nuts. He wrote that she flew into "prodigious Paroxysms" of rage against him and that he feared her madness would undermine his ministry.

As troubling and troubled as his wife was, Mather was also distressed by his son Increase, named for his grandfather and nicknamed "Cresy." Cotton Mather wrote more than four hundred books during his life on science, nature, and history, as well as on theology. Maybe he should have spent more time with his kids. Cresy was a wild young man. Eventually, Mather attempted to disown the troublemaker, but entries in his journals show that he forgave Cresy many times.

"My miserable, miserable Son Increase!" Mather wrote. "The wretch has brought himself under public Trouble and Infamy by bearing a part in a Night-Riot, with some detestable Rakes in the town."

In 1689 Mather published *Memorable Providences, Relating to Witchcrafts and Possessions,* detailing the possession of the four children of a Boston mason and the subsequent hanging of Irish washerwoman Goody Glover, "the witch" who was Roman Catholic and spoke "Irish" (Gaelic). In the introduction, Mather set the stage for the horrors to come in Salem three years later.

"Go tell Mankind, that there are Devils and Witches," he wrote, "and that tho those night-birds least appear where the Day-light of the Gospel comes, yet New-Engl. has had Exemples of their Existence and Operation; and that not only the Wigwams of Indians, where the pagan Powaws often raise their masters, in the shapes of Bears and Snakes and Fires, but the House of Christians, where our God has had his constant Worship, have undergone the Annoyance of Evil spirits."

Mather wrote that he visited Goody (short for Goodwife and the standard salutation for married women in Puritan Boston) Glover in jail and she was unable to recite the Lord's Prayer.

"When she was asked, Whether she believed there was a God? her Answer was too blasphemous and horrible for any Pen of mine to mention," Mather wrote. "An Experiment was made, Whether she could recite the Lords Prayer; and it was found, that tho clause after clause was most carefully repeated unto her, yet when she said it after them that prompted her, she could not Possibly avoid making Nonsense of it, with some ridiculous Depravations. This Experiment I had the curiosity since to see made upon two more, and it had the same Event."

Mather's *Memorable Providences, Relating to Witchcraft and Possession,* "displays a very extraordinary amount of credulity, and an equally great want of anything like sound judgment," wrote publisher John Russell Smith, who republished *Wonders of the Invisible World* in 1862. "This work, no doubt, spread the alarm of witchcraft through the whole colony, and had some influence, on the events which followed."

Memorable Providences became a much-discussed bestseller in Puritan New England and was among only a handful of books in the library of Samuel Parris, the Salem minister in whose house began the horrible events of 1692. It is almost certain that the girls who reported fits caused by witches in Salem had read Mather's book, which describes the Goodwin children's fits in detail. It is especially curious that among the nineteen alleged witches who were hung on Gallows Hill in the summer of 1692—the twentieth victim was an eighty-year-old man, Giles Corey, who was crushed between two large stones (after two days of refusing to confess, Corey's last words were "more weight")—one was a minister George Burroughs, whose main crime was a disbelief in witchcraft. Mather rode his horse to Salem to watch him hang. When Burroughs was able to recite the Lord's Prayer perfectly, some in the crowd called for the execution to be stopped. Mather—hypocrite that he was—intervened, reminding those gathered that Burroughs had been convicted by a jury. He conveniently chose to forget that he used Goody Goodwin's inability to recite the Lord's Prayer as damning evidence.

Mather was called out on his actions. Robert Calef was born in England in 1648 and came to Massachusetts around 1688. He gave his book criticizing the Salem Witchcraft Trials a sarcastic name, *More Wonders of the Invisible World* (1700). He especially denounced Cotton Mather for his insistence that spectral evidence (testimony regarding alleged actions and behavior by the accused that were invisible to all but the alleged victims) and demonic possessions could be documented.

Mather's defense of the Salem trials had first appeared in *The Wonders of the Invisible World* (1692), in which he supported the decision of the judges to admit "spectral evidence." The girls in Salem, for example, would fall to the floor of the courtroom, writhing in pain, and claim the accused had "sent out their spirits" to pinch them and stick them with needles. Even Increase Mather thought spectral evidence was bull.

"Only the same God who hath said, thou shalt not suffer a Witch to live; hath also said, at the Mouth of two Witnesses, or three Witnesses shall he that is worthy of Death, be put to Death: But at the Mouth of one Witness, he shall not be put to Death, Deut. 17. 6," Increase wrote in *A Case of Conscience*. "Much debate is made about what is sufficient Conviction, and some have (in their Zeal) supposed that a less clear evidence ought to pass in this than in other Cases, supposing that else it will be hard (if possible) to bring such to condign Punishment, by reason of the close conveyances that there are between the Devil and Witches; but this is a very dangerous and unjustifiable tenet."

The trials started out with the girls accusing people who lived on the edge of Salem's society—a slave from Barbados and a beggar woman— but soon other, more prominent figures were accused. The trials lasted less than a year and finally ended as a great embarrassment to Puritan society, which was already in its death throes.

"The witchcraft delusion had, however, been sufficiently dispelled to prevent the recurrence of any other such persecutions; and those who still insisted on their truth were restrained to the comparatively harmless publication and defense of their opinions," Smith wrote in 1862. "The people of Salem were humbled and repentant. They deserted their minister, Mr. Paris (sic), with whom the persecution had begun, and were not satisfied until they had driven him away from the place. Their remorse continued through several years, and most of the people concerned in the judicial proceedings proclaimed their regret. The jurors signed a paper expressing their repentance, and pleading that they had laboured under a delusion. What ought to have been considered still more conclusive, many of those who had confessed themselves witches, and had been instrumental in accusing others, retracted all they had said, and confessed that they had acted under the influence of terror. Yet the vanity of superior intelligence and knowledge was so great in the two Mathers that they resisted all conviction. In his *Magnalia,* an ecclesiastical history of New England, published in 1700, Cotton Mather repeats his original view of the doings of Satan in Salem, showing no regret for the part he had taken in this affair, and making no retraction of any of his opinions."

After the trials ended, Mather became involved in the cases of two "possessed" women and recorded his efforts to exorcise both Sarah Good and Margaret Rule. His accounts of these exorcisms remained unpublished, but Calef, who twice visited Rule while she was undergoing treatment, gained access to the Rule manuscript. He wrote and circulated his own version of the events, accusing both Cotton and Increase of pressuring Rule and influencing her report of her symptoms. Calef also accused the Mathers of engaging in overt sexual behavior such as rubbing Rule's stomach and breasts in order to ease her distress. Enraged, Increase Mather, then Harvard College president, burned Calef's book in Harvard Yard, and Cotton Mather denounced Calef from his pulpit and began a lawsuit against him.

Cotton Mather had some good qualities. He was forward thinking about the possibility of medicine and his intellect and courage saved many lives in 1721. Mather had survived smallpox when he was a child but the disease had claimed members of his own family. He had learned about inoculations through his correspondence with the Royal Society of London, and from his slave Onesimus. Onesimus showed Mather the scars on his arms where he had been inoculated in his native West Indies.

Courage

In April 1721 a fresh outbreak of smallpox swept through Boston. By May it had become an epidemic and people began fleeing the city.

"The grievous calamity of the smallpox has now entered the town," Mather wrote in his diary.

He also wrote a letter to the physicians of Boston urging inoculations for healthy Bostonians. The method used would be to take pus from a smallpox victim and introduce it into a healthy person's blood through a small incision. A short illness would then result in future immunity. All the physicians except one turned on Mather. The one was a young doctor named Zabdiel Boylston. Boylston inoculated his own son, the first inoculation ever to be administered in America, and the boy quickly recovered. He kept inoculating volunteers, including Mather's son Samuel, despite being called before the Magistrates and despite a public outcry against Mather and him. A bomb was even thrown through Mather's window, but the lit fuse was knocked off and it did not explode.

"They rave, they rail, they blaspheme, they talk not only like Ideots, but also like Fanaticks, and not only the physician who began the Experiment, but I also am the object of their fury," Mather wrote.

Of the 242 patients inoculated by Dr. Boylston, only six died. Of the 5,889 Bostonians who contracted smallpox, 884 of them died.

Two years after the smallpox epidemic, Cotton Mather's father Increase died at the age of eighty-four. The next year, Cotton's troublesome son Increase was lost at sea. Only two of his fifteen children remained alive. Cotton Mather never apologized for his role in the witch trials in Salem or in Boston. He never changed his view on Native Americans and he forever became the dour face of the harsh religion, which still influences New England thought and law today. By the early eighteenth century, though—even in Massachusetts during Mather's lifetime—Puritanism itself was fading.

In late 1727, Cotton Mather became ill and his condition quickly worsened over the next two months. His son Samuel asked him for his final thoughts. Mather said, "Remember only that one word, Fructuosus," ("fruitful" in Latin). He died the day after his sixty-fifth birthday, on February 13, 1728.

CHAPTER 2

Thomas Hutchinson
"One of the most hated men on earth"

Thomas Hutchinson was the last civilian royal governor of the Massachusetts colony. He was also a colossal waffle, a loyalist who professed to love both his native Massachusetts and English governance, not a great position to take in Boston, the Cradle of Liberty, in the late 1760s and early 1770s.

Still acknowledged as a great historian, smarmy rich kid Hutchinson chose the wrong side and so goes down in history as possibly the most reviled man ever in Beantown.

"A thought of independence I could not think it possible should enter into the heart of any man in his senses," he wrote in 1766.

Eight years later, Hutchinson was on a slow boat to London, forced out of his beloved Massachusetts by men who believed "a thought of independence" not only sensible, but a great and noble idea too. In one of the many ironies that marked his life, on the fourth of July, 1776, he received an honorary doctorate in civil law from Oxford University. Hutchinson claimed he valued that honor above all others.

"Certainly none so fittingly symbolizes the tragedy of his life," wrote Harvard University historian Bernard Bailyn. "But to the people who on the day of Hutchinson's award proclaimed their nation's independence, he was one of the most hated men on earth."

Pretty much everyone in colonial Massachusetts—except for his wife and children—thought Hutchinson was a jerk. Firebrands Samuel Adams, James Otis, and Joseph Warren thought he was a lackey for Parliament's unfair tax policies, and they loved to use him as a target for scorn.

"We have for a long time known your enmity to this Province. We have had full proof of your cruelty to a loyal people. No age has, perhaps, furnished a more glaring instance of obstinate perseverance in the path of malice," Warren, a twenty-seven-year-old physician, wrote about then Lieutenant Governor Hutchinson in the *Boston Gazette* on February 29, 1768. "We never can treat good and patriotic rulers with too great reverence. But it is certain that men totally abandoned to wickedness can never merit our regard, be their stations ever so high. If such men are by God appointed, the Devil may be the Lord's anointed."

Using a pen name, as was the style of the day, Warren signed his letter "A True Patriot."

Meanwhile British Prime Minister Lord North thought Hutchinson's waffling was a significant contributor to the tensions that led to the outbreak of the American Revolutionary War. That is an opinion shared by historian Bailyn, whose *The Ordeal of Thomas Hutchinson* won the National Book Award in 1974 and is a sympathetic and tragic portrayal of Hutchinson, a circumspect and cautious conservative caught in the maelstrom of social upheaval.

"If there was one person in America whose actions might have altered the outcome" of the events preceding the American Revolutionary War, Bailyn wrote, "it was he."

Hutchinson was born the son of a wealthy merchant and he stayed wealthy. He never quite viewed the world through the same lens as the working-class Bostonians whom he would come to call "the rabble." His great-great-grandmother was Anne Hutchinson, who was expelled from the Massachusetts Bay Colony in 1638 after antagonizing Boston Puritan religious leaders, including first Governor John Winthrop, by challenging their religious views. When she and five of her children died in a massacre by the Mohegans on Long Island in 1643, her male adversaries back in Beantown saw it as divine justice.

"God's hand is the more apparently seen herein, to pick this woeful woman, to make her and those belonging to her an unheard of heavy example," Puritan minister the Reverend Thomas Weld pronounced.

Governor Thomas Hutchinson

BENSON J. LOSSING, *THE PICTORIAL FIELD-BOOK OF THE REVOLUTION*, NEW YORK: HARPER & BROTHERS, 1852

Because of her liberal views, Anne Hutchinson has often been called America's first feminist. Her great-great-grandson was just the opposite. When he was sent packing to Mother England in 1774, it was because he was too conservative. With cries of "Liberty" echoing through the streets of Boston, Hutchinson continued to suckle at the teat of Mother England. He stood proudly on the wrong side of history and didn't back down. He blamed all the problems leading to the American Revolution on "incendiaries" like Samuel Adams.

"Americans were convinced in their own minds that they were very miserable, and those who think so are so," he wrote after the Revolution. "There is nothing so easy as to persuade people that they are badly governed. Take happy and comfortable people and talk to them with the art of the evil one, and they can soon be made discontented with their government, their rulers, with everything around them, and even with themselves."

Hutchinson was born on September 9, 1711, in Boston's North End, the fourth of twelve children of Colonel Thomas and Sarah Foster Hutchinson. His parents were both from well-to-do merchant families that had helped found New England and, as it grew, so did their fortunes. "They were accumulators, down to earth, unromantic middle men, whose solid petty bourgeois characteristics became steadily more concentrated in the passage of the years until in Thomas, in the fifth generation, they reached an apparently absolute and perfect form," Bailyn wrote.

Hutchinson's early years were marked by family tragedy, foreshadowing similar family tragedies in his adult life. His older brother Foster died at seventeen from a smallpox inoculation, followed by the death of an infant brother and young sister, who died of consumption (tuberculosis). His twenty-three-year-old brother Elisha died from fever in 1739. That "broke his [father's] heart" Hutchinson would later write, and Colonel Thomas died shortly afterward.

Hutchinson had entered Harvard College when he was twelve and graduated when he was just fifteen. His father got him started in business and he thrived. By the time he was in his mid-twenties, he had already made his fortune. In 1734 he married Margaret "Peggy" Sanford, a distant relative and the granddaughter of Rhode Island Governor Peleg Sanford. Their marriage was a joyous one and they could not bear to be apart. She gave birth to twelve children—only five of whom survived infancy. Margaret's final words when she died in childbirth in 1754, uttered with "her dying voice and eyes fixed on me," Hutchinson wrote were "best of husbands." Hutchinson named the baby "Peggy" in her honor.

Three years after his marriage, Hutchinson began his political career. He was elected a Boston selectman and member of the General Council in 1737. He set the tone for his political career by advocating against paper currency and pushing a proposal through the council that money in the colony would be based on British silver. The working class and poor favored paper currency and "the rabble" never forgave Hutchinson for that. He continued as a loyal member of the colonial government under appointed royal governors William Shirley, Thomas Pownall, and Francis Bernard. His relationship with the common people would get worse when he became chief justice and lieutenant governor. Although he did not advocate for the Stamp Tax, Sugar Tax, or Townshend Acts, he did not think the colonies had any right to resist English Parliament. The "rabble" paid him back by ransacking his Boston house during the Stamp Act Crisis in 1765.

"I often think," he wrote during that crisis, "how quiet and contented I was before I quitted my mercantile life for a political one, and it adds to my misfortune that from my present station I cannot return to my former condition with honor."

Hutchinson personally disapproved of the hated Stamp Act, which placed a heavy tax on all published materials, other than books, in the colonies. Parliament levied the tax, the first aimed at only the colonies, to pay for the just-ended French and Indian War, and to maintain an army in America. Hutchinson thought the tax was unfair since the crown had given American colonies the right to levy their own taxes, and because they had no true representation in Parliament. He also believed, however, that the colonies could not survive without the protection of the English military and said it was better to "submit to some abridgment of our rights than to break off our connection."

Bay State patriots, calling for "no taxation without representation," would have none of Hutchinson's waffling.

"We have always understood it to be a grand and fundamental principle of the [English] constitution that no freeman should be subject to any tax to which he has not given his own consent," wrote John Adams. The colonists accused Hutchinson of treason and secretly trying to promote passage of the Stamp Act and they went wild when Hutchinson's brother-in-law, Andrew Oliver, was announced as the new stamp master. The newspapers in Boston were soon filled with vitriolic anonymous letters attacking Hutchinson and accusing him of writing to England in favor of the Stamp Act.

"The people, brooding over the injury they had received in the Stamp Act, became fiercer in temper," wrote nineteenth-century biographer James Hosmer. "The rough population which abounded about the wharves and shipyards grew riotous, and, with the usual want of discrimination shown by mobs, were not slow to lift their hands against even their best friends. Andrew Oliver . . . was hung in effigy, a drunken crowd carrying the effigy through the Town-House, even while the Governor and Council were in session in the chamber above. Oliver's house was attacked, until at last he made public recantation."

On August 14, 1765, a crowd surrounded Hutchinson's house and demanded he declare publicly that he never wrote to promote the Stamp Act. They left without violence but returned twelve days later.

Hutchinson was having dinner with his children when a mob appeared on August 26. The family fled the house as the rioters used axes to smash in the doors and break up the furniture. The rioters broke down the inner walls, stole 900 pounds sterling, and all the plates and clothing in the house. They scattered the pages of Hutchinson's *History of Massachusetts Bay* manuscript and the books in his library. They spent hours trying to tear down the home's cupola.

"Such ruin was never seen in America," Hutchinson wrote in a letter. "The encouragers of the first mob never intended matters should go this length, and the people in general expressed the utmost detestation of this unparalleled outrage, and I wish they could be convinced what infinite hazard there is of the most terrible consequences from such demons, when they are let loose in a government where there is not constant authority at hand sufficient to suppress them."

The next day, a shaken and tearful Hutchinson appeared in court without his robes. He addressed the court: "I call on my Maker to witness that I never, in New England or in Old, in Great Britain or in America, neither directly nor indirectly, was aiding, assisting, supporting or in the least promoting or encouraging what is commonly called the Stamp Act."

Hutchinson's family moved to their summer home in Milton, just south of Boston and overlooking the Neponset River. It was a place he had long loved. He later described it to King George III in 1774 this way:

"My house is seven or eight miles from town, a pleasant situation, and many gentlemen from abroad say it has the finest prospect from it they ever saw, except where great improvements have been made by art, to help the natural view."

By the late 1760s, Hutchinson's enemies in Massachusetts had increased in number and in boldness, and rebellion was in the air. Hutchinson continued to try to walk a fine line that was no longer there. "He tried to reconcile king and colony, but neither was in a mood to be reconciled," according to 1907's *The Cambridge History of English and American Literature.*

The Stamp Act was repealed in 1766, but on the same day Parliament passed the Declaratory Act, asserting its right to bind the colonies by its laws. The following year, Parliament passed the Townshend Acts in an effort to raise more revenue from the colonies. When John Hancock's sloop *Liberty* arrived in Boston with a cargo of wine in 1768, a customs official was held hostage as the wine was unloaded without payment of the required duties. The *Liberty* was seized, and rioters attacked customs officials. Two regiments of British regulars landed in Boston to deal with the growing unrest.

The quartering of the British troops enraged Bostonians. Sam Adams and other anonymous newspaper contributors—think of them as colonial bloggers—began reporting that the Redcoats were raping young women and beating boys. Even Sam Adams's dog, a big Newfoundland named Queue, hated the sight of the Redcoats patrolling Boston streets.

"[Queue] had a vast antipathy to the British uniform," Hosmer wrote. "He was cut and shot in several places by soldiers, in retaliation for his own sharp attacks, for the patriotic Queue anticipated the 'embattled farmers' of Concord Bridge in inaugurating hostilities, and bore to his grave honourable scars from his fierce encounters."

Bernard had resigned as governor of Massachusetts in 1769 and Hutchinson became acting governor. According to Bailyn, at the start of 1770 "[Hutchinson] was convinced that an explosion between the soldiers in Boston and the populace was likely. Though he himself had welcomed the troops to Boston as the only means of maintaining order . . . he knew the dangers of their presence."

The enmity came to a head on March 5, 1770, when British soldiers fired into a jeering crowd that was throwing snowballs, pieces of ice, and oyster shells at them. Five colonists died. Hutchinson rushed to the scene and implored the crowd to be calm.

"It is certain that nothing more unfortunate could have happened, for a very great part of the people were in a perfect frenzy by means of it," he later wrote.

Sam Adams and the Boston selectmen demanded Hutchinson remove the troops from town or promised they would drive them out with "blood and carnage." Hutchinson acquiesced and the troops were removed to present day Castle Island in Boston Harbor. Eight British enlisted men and their commander, Captain Thomas Preston, were tried for murder. John Adams—citing the doctrine that all accused deserved legal counsel—led the defense team and just two privates were found guilty of manslaughter.

The Boston Massacre became a rallying point for the patriots in the next five years leading up to the War of Independence.

"[Hutchinson] concluded as soon as the immediate shock of the Massacre passed there was little to hope for," Bailyn wrote. "The Massacre, he knew, would be used by the opposition to brand him a bloodthirsty tyrant."

The revolutionary spirit and hatred of Hutchinson surged over the ensuing years. Hutchinson was appointed governor in 1771 despite his effort to avoid it. (The official appointment and his letter declining it passed in ships on the Atlantic.)

In June 1773 Benjamin Franklin discovered thirteen letters that Hutchinson had sent to England in 1768 and 1769, recommending that self-governance be taken away from the colonies "by degree," and that there should be "abridgement of what are called English liberties." Franklin sent the letters to Boston newspapers and their publication further enflamed the patriotic colonists' hatred of Hutchinson. In December 1773, in response to a new oppressive tax on tea, the Sons of Liberty dressed up as Mohegan Indians and held the infamous Boston Tea Party in Boston Harbor.

By 1774, Hutchinson was suffering from depression. He was the most hated man in all the colonies—he was even burned in effigy in Philadelphia. When his brother-in-law Andrew Oliver died, a mob hooted at his funeral procession in Boston. The Massachusetts colony was out of control and military governor General Thomas Gage replaced Hutchinson.

On May 30, 1774, friendly merchants, neighbors, and clergymen published testimonials to Hutchinson in Boston newspapers next to columns that bade farewell to "the disgraced and execrated TRAITOR."

The next day, Hutchinson, along with his daughter Peggy and son Elisha, boarded the *Minerva* for England. They left behind a province in open rebellion.

In England, Hutchinson advised King George about the colonies and received his doctorate and other honors. He had hoped to return to his native Massachusetts in months, but relations between the old world and new only worsened. Hutchinson tried to caution the British to stop punishing Massachusetts, but found no audience. In April 1775, the world heard the shots fired in Lexington and Concord. Mobs harassed Hutchinson's loyalist family still in Massachusetts, and his beloved house in Milton was turned into a barracks for the Continental Army.

Meanwhile, Hutchinson grew increasingly miserable in England. His cherished daughter Peggy died in September 1777 after a long illness, and he wrote friends that his grief was even more complete than when his wife had passed. When England's old enemy France joined the American cause in 1778, he wrote, "Everybody is struck dumb."

Hutchinson still longed to return to his home, but in 1779 he received notification that he was listed in the Acts of Banishment as the first of "conspirators against the liberties of the people," barring him forever from Massachusetts and confiscating all his property there.

Within months, his son Billy died. Hutchinson himself suffered a stroke and died on June 3, 1780, the same month the Massachusetts Constitution, penned by old rival John Adams, went into effect. Hutchinson's third volume of *The History of Massachusetts Bay* was published posthumously.

In his *The Ordeal of Thomas Hutchinson,* Bailyn asks, "Who were the losers of the American Revolution?" Not the British, he said. Yes, they lost the war and part of their empire, but they did not lose their government or rights, and their way of life certainly benefited from continued trade with the former colonies.

"The real losers—those whose lives were disrupted, who suffered violence and vilification, who were driven out . . . and died grieving for the homes they had lost . . . they were the American loyalists," Bailyn wrote. And Thomas Hutchinson, he added, was "the most important loyalist of all."

CHAPTER 3

Dr. Benjamin Church
"Make use of every precaution or I perish"

Less than seven months after the first shots in the War for Independence were fired at the Battle of Lexington, John Adams, in Philadelphia with the Continental Congress, received two astonishing letters from friends near Boston.

On September 30, William Tudor wrote from Cambridge, "To our great Astonishment the Surgeon General was this forenoon put under an Arrest for Corresponding with the Army in Boston. An intercepted Letter wrote in Characters, and some other Circumstances, have made the Suspicions very strong against him. His House has been search'd and all his Papers seiz'd, by the General's Orders. I am not now acquainted with any farther Particulars. You will doubtless have the fullest Information sent the Congress from Head Quarters. Good God! Doctor C——h proves a Traitor! What a Triumph to the Tories?"

The next day, fellow patriot James Warren in Watertown sent the future president even more information.

"My Dear Sir," Warren wrote. "An Event has lately taken place here, which makes much Noise, and gives me much Uneasiness not only as it Affects the Character, and may prove the ruin of a Man who I used to have a Tolerable Opinion of, but as it may be the Cause of many suspicions and Jealousies and what is still worse, have a Tendency to discredit the Recommendations of my Friends at the Congress. Dr. C——h has been detected in a Correspondence with the Enemy."

Dr. C——h was Dr. Benjamin Church, an esteemed patriot leader, the American army's first surgeon general, and, as it turned out, America's first traitor.

Church was born in Newport, Rhode Island, on August 24, 1734. He was the great grandson of Colonel Benjamin Church, the English colonist hero of King Philip's War. His father, also Benjamin, was a deacon in Mather Byles's church in Boston.

Young Benjamin graduated from Boston Latin School and then Harvard College in 1754. He was not only a doctor, but also a poet, and two of his poems appeared in a collection celebrating the accession of George III. He studied medicine with Dr. Joseph Pynchon and traveled to London where he married Sarah Hill of Ross, Herefordshire. It turns out he continued to enjoy the company of other women, too, which was part of his downfall.

He joined Sam Adams, John Adams, and other Whigs in resisting the Stamp Act and other British taxes and oppressive measures, and he seemed a full-fledged patriot. In a poem "To the King," he succinctly expressed the colonists' desires:

Long live the great King George in peace and harmony
Of his fame we will sing, if we have liberty
But if cut short of that we cannot raise our voice
For hearts full of regret can never rejoice.

By 1765, Boston was already afire with rebellion. The Stamp Act Riots included the total trashing of Royal Lieutenant Governor and Chief Justice Thomas Hutchinson's home, by "the rough population which abounded about the wharves and shipyards," according to nineteenth-century historian James K. Hosmer. The same mob had earlier sacked the home of Hutchinson's brother-in-law, Stamp Master Andrew Oliver, hung Oliver in effigy, and nine years later, in 1774, jeered when Oliver's funeral procession winded through the streets of Boston. "America is a mere bully, from one end to the other, and the Bostonians by far the greatest bullies," British commander of all forces in North America, General Thomas Gage, later wrote in a letter to a friend.

"As resistance grew into mob violence, Gage began to think that the trouble arose not from the mobs themselves, but from colonial elites who set the rioters in motion," David Hackett Fischer wrote in his 1994 book *Paul Revere's Ride*. "In company with others of his rank, he believed that the 'lower orders,' or the 'inferior people,' as he described the vast majority of humanity, were of no political importance. After the Stamp Act Riots, he wrote, 'The plan of the people of property, is to raise the lower class to prevent the execution of the Law. . . . The lawyers are the source from which these clamors have flowed . . . merchants in general, assembly men, magistrates, &c have been united in this plan of riots, and without the influence and instigation of these the inferior people would have been quiet. . . . The sailors who are the only people who may be properly stiled [sic] Mob, are entirely at the command of the Merchants who employ them.'"

The growing dissatisfaction of the Massachusetts colonists with Britain came to a head in 1770 while Bostonians were being forced to quarter two regiments of British troops. Among the troops quartered in the city was the 29th Regiment of Foot, which had previously clashed with colonists in Quebec and New York, and had a reputation for poor discipline. Bostonians hated their uninvited and unwanted armed guests. Sam Adams and others fueled that hatred with pieces published under pseudonyms in the *Boston Gazette, Boston Spy,* and other Whig-leaning newspapers accusing the British soldiers of rape, the beating of young boys, and failing to observe the Sabbath.

On March 5, 1770, British soldiers in the 29th fired into a crowd that was jeering them and throwing snowballs, pieces of ice, and oyster shells at them. Five colonists died. Church was the first physician to reach the scene and treat the wounded. Eight British enlisted men and their commander were tried for murder but just two privates were found guilty of manslaughter. Church and others made sure, however, that the Boston Massacre became a rallying point for the patriots in the next five years leading up to the Revolutionary War.

"Dr. Church was selected to present the oration celebrating the third anniversary of the Boston Massacre," David Potter and

Gordon Thomas wrote in *The Colonial Idiom.* "Delivered in the Old South Church on March 5, 1773, it was received 'with universal applause.' So big a crowd attended the ceremony that John Hancock, acting as moderator, had to be helped through a window so that he might reach his place on the platform."

In his speech, Church railed against the British, condemned the king, and called for liberty from the crown.

"Kings, the servants of the state, when they degenerate into tyrants, forfeit their right to government," Church thundered. "A BREACH of trust in a governor, or attempting to enlarge a limited power; effectually absolves subjects from every bond of covenant and peace; the crimes acted by a King against the people, are the highest treason against the highest law among men."

Those in attendance that day would later be shocked that Church was almost certainly already on the payroll of Gage. "The old Sons of Liberty, Long Room, North Caucus, and Masonic crowd were paralyzed with amazement," when Church's duplicity was revealed two years later, Esther Forbes wrote in her Pulitzer Prize–winning *Paul Revere and the World He Lived In.*

Gage had been seeking an ally from among the "people of property." He tried to bribe Sam Adams in 1773, who, although always broke, responded, "Go tell General Gage that my peace has long since been made with the King of kings, and that it is the advice of Samuel Adams to him, no longer to insult the feelings of an already exasperated people."

Gage had a lot better luck with Church, who was broke from building a lavish summer home in Raynham in 1768 and from maintaining his "kept women" on the side. Historians are not certain when Church started spying for Gage, but almost all agree it was probably before 1772, maybe even before 1770.

"It was amazing his associates did not see through him earlier," Forbes wrote. "Doctor Church was a witty, lively fellow who after taking his degree at Harvard, had gone to England to 'walk' the London hospitals. . . . He was high-strung, bombastic, always hard up and known for supporting a mistress. . . . There was something queer about Doctor Church. Paul Revere felt it, and so did Joseph Warren."

Church did much of his spying while on a committee formed by Paul Revere in 1774 "for the purpose of watching the movements of the British soldiers, and gaining every intelligence of the movements of the Tories," Revere later wrote. The informal group of unemployed artisans and workmen watched every move of the troops and then reported what they saw when the committee met at the Green Dragon Tavern in Boston. If the troops or Loyalists did anything out of the ordinary, Revere sent word to Dr. Joseph Warren, who forwarded the news to the colonists' committee of safety in Concord.

"We were so careful that our meetings should be kept secret," Revere later wrote, "that every time we met, every person swore upon the Bible that he would not discover any of our transactions but to Messrs Hancock, Adams, Doctors Warren, Church and one or two more."

Despite the precautions, Gage, who replaced Thomas Hutchinson as governor of Boston in 1774, knew everything the secret committee was up to.

"His source was Dr. Benjamin Church, who sat in the highest councils of the Whig movement, and betrayed it for money," Fischer wrote. "Many years later, Paul Revere remembered that 'a gentleman who had connections with the Tory party, but was a Whig at heart, acquainted me that our meetings were discovered, and mentioned the identical words that were spoken among us the night before.' Paul Revere's mechanics were unable to discover who was betraying them, and began to suspect one another. All the while they continued to report their activities to Dr. Benjamin Church, never imagining that Church himself was the traitor."

The night of April 18, 1775, was chilly but the early spring of that year had been unusually warm, and fruit trees were already blossoming. About one thousand British regulars marched from Boston to Lexington to arrest Samuel Adams and John Hancock, and to seize the colonists' store of weapons and gunpowder in Concord. Most of the munitions had been moved days before: Gage had his spy and the Americans had theirs—probably Gage's own American-born wife Margaret Kemble Gage who was feeding Dr. Warren information. Paul Revere on his legendary ride arrived just before the Redcoats to alarm the countryside.

The next morning, two lines of "embattled farmers," about seventy men under Captain John Parker, awaited seven hundred regulars from the mightiest army in the world under Major John Pitcairn. "Stand your ground; don't fire unless fired upon, but if they mean to have a war, let it begin here," Parker has been famously quoted as telling his men.

"They there halted," Minuteman Sylvanus Wood recalled of the British approach to Lexington's Town Green years later. "The officer then swung his sword, and said, 'Lay down your arms, you damned rebels, or you are all dead men. Fire!' Some guns were fired by the British at us from the first platoon, but no person was killed or hurt, being probably charged only with powder. Just at this time, Captain Parker ordered every man to take care of himself. The company immediately dispersed; and while the company was dispersing and leaping over the wall, the second platoon of the British fired and killed some of our men."

The first shot—it has never been definitively determined which side fired it—was unleashed just as the sun was rising. Eight militiamen were killed, nine wounded, and the outnumbered colonists quickly fell back. The British army marched west to Concord, but found few weapons. At the North Bridge, the reinforced militia—now numbering in the thousands—defeated three companies of Redcoats. Minutemen continued to pour in from the surrounding countryside—Woburn, Carlisle, Chelmsford, Westford, Sudbury, and beyond—and the British turned and retreated toward Charlestown, being harassed by the Americans the entire seventeen miles. When they reached Boston, the Redcoats put the town in lockdown and the residents still there were trapped between the Charles River and the British fleet in Boston Harbor.

The morning after Concord and Lexington, Church showed up in Cambridge with a bloody sock—perhaps the second most famous bloody sock in Boston history behind the one the Red Sox's Curt Schilling wore while beating the Yankees in the 2004 play-offs. Church, who Revere and others already privately suspected, was with Dr. Joseph Warren, who had been grazed by a bullet as he joined the harassment of the retreating British troops.

"Doctor Benjamin Church's battle scars were even less impressive than Doctor Warren's," Forbes wrote. "Paul Revere met him and noticed his bloody stockings. The physician said he had been in yesterday's battle. The man next to him had been killed and his blood spurted on him. This might well have humbled Revere, who does not seem to have been anywhere near the fighting—and possibly was eating salmon instead. 'I argued with myself, if a man will risk his life for a cause, he must be a friend to that cause; and I never suspected him after, till he was charged with being a traitor.'"

The next day, Revere, Warren, and the other American leaders began planning what to do next, as thousands of Minutemen eager to fight the British were pouring into Cambridge.

"Doctor Church suddenly jumped to his feet and threw a bombshell," Forbes wrote. "'Doctor Warren, I am determined to go to Boston tomorrow.' Not a man in the room could openly go to Boston without risking death. Paul Revere says that Church's sudden statement 'set them all a-staring.' He knew at this time that 'Doctor Warren had not the greatest affection for him' and 'I must say I never thought him a man of principle' but he recollected the blood upon his stockings. Dr. Church had risked his life for the cause. He must be a friend to it."

The patriots came up with a plan that Church would say he needed to go into Boston to get medical supplies. He drove into Boston in a carriage and returned two days later. He claimed he had been taken prisoner and brought before Gage, who pressed him for information before he released him. One Bostonian, however, later told Revere he had seen Church and the general "discoursing together, like persons who had long been acquainted," and another said that he saw Church going into Gage's home, "more like a man that was acquainted than a prisoner."

While her husband organized the rebel cause in Cambridge, Rachel Revere remained in Boston, one of the residents trapped between the British troops guarding the bridges along the Charles and the warships in the harbor.

"She was less concerned about her own fate than about the safety of her husband," Fischer wrote. "After the battle he managed to get a message to her, but Rachel continued to worry that he had nothing to live on but the charity of his many friends."

Rachel Revere decided to smuggle money to her husband with Church. She included this letter:

> *My dear by Doctor Church I send a hundred and twenty-five pounds & beg you will take the best care of yourself & not attempt coming into this towne again & if I have an opportunity of coming or sending out anything or any of the children I shall do it. Pray keep up your spirits & trust yourself & us in the hands of a good God who will take care of us. Tis all my dependence, for vain is the help of man. Adieu my love. from your Affectionate R. Revere.*

Rachel Revere's message never reached her husband. Two centuries later it turned up in a trunk of General Gage's papers discovered in Sussex, England.

"One wonders what happened to the money," Fischer wrote.

The lives of doctors Church and Warren would quickly take different paths. Two months after the fighting in Lexington and Concord, Dr. Warren responded to the Battle of Bunker Hill. Not officially commissioned yet as a major general, Warren insisted on fighting on the front lines as an infantryman and was killed.

In May, George Washington arrived in Massachusetts to take command of the Continental Army. He made Church the first Surgeon General and Chief Physician of the army's hospital in Cambridge in July.

Engraving of the Boston Massacre by Paul Revere

Within three months, though, Church's treachery was discovered. He had given his mistress a letter in cipher to give to a British officer in Boston, which was now under siege by 16,000 American troops. She had left it with a baker, Godfrey Wainwood, in Newport, Rhode Island, who promised to deliver it. The patriotic Wainwood instead gave the letter to American authorities. George Washington asked Eldridge Gerry and another code breaker to decipher it independently. They both quickly reached the same conclusion: Church was feeding Gage information on Colonial troop strength. The letter ended with "Make use of every precaution or I perish."

Washington put Church on trial before the Provincial Congress in Watertown. Church admitted writing the letter but claimed he had intentionally overstated the rebel's strength to deceive Gage.

"The galleries were packed," Forbes wrote. "He defended himself pretty well but seems to have been guilty beyond any reasonable doubt. In vain now, his rolling eyes and poetic fancies, his 'the warmest bosom here does not flame with a brighter zeal for security, happiness, liberty of America' and so on."

The Americans he had betrayed were furious. Abigail Adams wrote to John Adams, "You may well hope to bind up a hungry tiger with a cobweb as to hold such debauched patriots in the visionary chains of decency."

Washington wrote this report to the President of Congress:

I have now a painful though necessary duty to perform, respecting Doctor Church, the Director of the Hospital. About a week ago, Mr. Secretary Ward, of Providence, sent up one Wainwood, an inhabitant of Newport, to me with a letter directed to Major Cane in Boston, in occult letters, which he said had been left with Wainwood some time ago by a woman who was kept by Doctor Church. . . . He, suspecting some improper correspondence, kept the letter and after some time opened it, but not being able to read it, laid it up, where it remained until he received an obscure letter from the woman, expressing an anxiety as to the original letter. He then communicated the whole matter to Mr. Ward, who sent him up with the papers to me. I immediately secured the woman, but for a long time she was proof against every threat and persuasion to discover the author. However she was at length brought to a confession and named Doctor Church. I then immediately secured him and all his papers. Upon the first examination he readily acknowledged the letter and said that it was designed for his brother, etc. The army and country are exceedingly irritated.

It was so early in the Revolution that no penalties for treason or spying had been put into place. Instead of a firing squad or gallows—from which later-discovered traitors such as Major John Andre, a confederate of Benedict Arnold, did swing—Church was expelled from the Massachusetts Provincial House of Representatives and sent to jail in Norwich, Connecticut, "debarred of use of pen and paper."

In 1777 an angry mob ransacked Church's home in Boston, forcing Sarah and their three children to flee America, sailing first to France and then England. In January 1778, in ill health with asthma, Church was allowed to leave his native land. He boarded the sloop *Welcome,* bound for the West Indies. The *Welcome* sank in a New England coastal storm. All hands, including America's first traitor, perished. His family received a pension from the British government.

CHAPTER 4

Professor John W. Webster
"Our professors do not often commit murder"

In 1850 a murder trial as sensational as any ever held in the United States focused international attention on Boston. The Parkman slaying was what journalists today, and probably even then, would call a "good murder," involving wealth, celebrity, intrigue, and a gruesome crime. Dr. John W. Webster, a chemistry and mineralogy professor at Harvard, stood accused of killing Dr. George Parkman, one of the richest men in Boston, over a debt, and then dismembering his body in his laboratory and burning parts of it in a furnace.

The case was one of the first using forensic evidence—Parkman's remains were ultimately identified by his dentures—and Judge Lemuel Shaw's controversial charge to the jury helped established the principle that "reasonable certainty" was sufficient for a conviction.

"The trial before the Supreme Judicial Court . . . was 'a cause of intense excitement, extending through the whole length and breadth of the land, and reaching even into foreign countries,'" Leonard Levy wrote in *The Law of the Commonwealth and Chief Justice Shaw* in 1986. "The device of changing the courtroom audience every ten minutes permitted sixty thousand people to glimpse the proceedings. Jared Sparks, historian-president of Harvard, one of a long parade of eminent character witnesses for Webster, commented, 'Our professors do not often commit murder.' But the evidence showed that [Webster] indubitably had."

The international fascination attached to the trial may not have been matched until the O. J. Simpson murder trial in 1995. Transcripts of the Webster trial proceedings—utilizing the new technology of "phonographic recording"—were rushed into print and the sensational Boston murder dominated the nation's newspapers for months. Even before the trial started, Bostonians and the rest of the country were debating Webster's guilt. The debate was often marked by class distinctions. Initially, police suspected Parkman's disappearance was the work of immigrants from famine-plagued Ireland who had swarmed into the city in recent years. Others came to suspect the prosecution's star witness, Ephraim Littlefield, a low-class "Swamp Yankee," who was the janitor at Harvard Medical School where the murder took place. Newspapers in the mid-nineteenth century made little pretense of objectivity and often took sides.

"The American Papers are making the most of the recent mysterious case of assassination at Boston," the *London Times* reported on December 27, 1849. *"The New York Herald,* now before us, has three columns of details on the subject. One of the local papers professes to discover in the evidence since adduced some 'developments' rather favourable to Professor Webster, the supposed murderer; but a minute analysis of all the circumstances hitherto brought to light induces us fully to concur in the remark of the *Boston Herald* that if Professor Webster be innocent of the crime of murder, the conspiracy of which he is made the victim is one of the most hellish on record."

John White Webster was born in 1793, the only child in a Boston family well connected to the upper class people who would come to be called the Boston Brahmins. Webster's mother was a Leverett, and his future wife was an in-law of the Prescotts. Murder victim George Parkman also belonged to this upper echelon of society, which initially helped to cast doubt on Webster's culpability among class-conscious Bostonians.

"In short, [Webster was] not the kind of man one would instinctively place among the criminal classes," Harvard professor Simon Schama wrote in *Dead Certainties, Unwarranted Speculations,* his 1991 historic fiction book about the trial.

Webster's grandfather had made the family fortune as a Boston merchant. Even though the family was rich, Webster's father, a pharmacist, kept young John on a tight allowance. Webster later blamed that—along with his desire to give his wife and four daughters everything they desired—as the reason he had difficulty as an adult handling money.

Webster graduated from Harvard Medical College in 1815, traveled to England, and then to the Azores, where he practiced medicine and married Harriet Hickling. The Websters returned to Boston and the doctor established a private medical practice, but the business end was a challenge for him as he always lived beyond his means. When his father died, Webster found out the family fortune was all but gone. To supplement his income, he became a lecturer in chemistry at Harvard Medical College in 1824 and was promoted to professor three years later. By 1849, he was making $1,200 a year, part of that from students buying tickets to his lectures.

According to "Murder at Harvard" on the PBS American Experience website: "At the same time, he and his wife created a place for themselves among the elite in Cambridge society. Accounts of Webster's character reveal that he was more talented in society than the lecture room. While he was described by all his friends as affable, well-spoken, charming and entertaining to have at a party, some did not speak so highly of him as a chemistry professor. . . . *The Boston Daily Bee* described Professor Webster as 'tolerated rather than respected, and has only retained his position on account of its comparative insignificance. As a lecturer he was dull and common-place and while the students took tickets to his lectures, they did not generally attend them.'"

By 1849 Dr. George Parkman was pretty much a doctor in name only. Also a Brahmin and scion of a wealthy Boston merchant, Parkman graduated from Harvard Medical College in 1809, six years ahead of Webster. He went to Europe to study further and while in France, visited an asylum for the insane. Upon his return to Boston in 1813, he became obsessed with building a humane asylum in Boston. He wrote two papers, "Remarks on Insanity" and "The Management of Lunatics," to publicize his ideas. He also raised money to buy land for the McLean Asylum for the Insane, but was bitterly disappointed when he was not appointed as its head. He quit practicing medicine, although he continued to visit the insane and even opened his Beacon Hill mansion to the ill during an outbreak of smallpox. He took over the family real estate business when his father died in 1824. Parkman was good at business—he bought vast amounts of land and real estate in Boston, including many dilapidated tenements. He also lent money.

Oliver Wendell Holmes Sr., fellow Brahmin, Harvard professor, and father of the future US Supreme Court justice, called Parkman the perfect Yankee: "He abstained while others indulged, he walked while others rode, he worked while others slept," Holmes wrote.

Parkman donated land for the Harvard Medical School (where Massachusetts General Hospital is today) and was seen by his blue-blooded friends as a philanthropist. He helped Webster get his appointment as lecturer. Fanny Longfellow, wife of the poet Henry Wadsworth Longfellow, called him "a good-natured Don Quixote." Others saw him as an unmerciful businessman—one impoverished woman told a newspaper reporter that on the day he disappeared Parkman tried to snatch a dollar intended for groceries from her hand when he came to collect her rent and she asked for more time.

"Dr. Parkman was a well-known figure in the streets of Boston," H. B. Irving wrote in the 1918 *A Book of Remarkable Criminals*. "His peculiar personal appearance and eccentric habits combined to make him something of a character. As he walked through the streets he presented a remarkable appearance. He was exceptionally tall, longer in the body than the legs; his lower jaw protruded some half an inch beyond the upper; he carried his body bent forward from the small of his back. He seemed to be always in a hurry; so impetuous was he that, if his horse did not travel fast enough to please him, he would get off its back, and, leaving the steed in the middle of the street, hasten on his way on foot. A just and generous man, he was extremely punctilious in matters of business, and uncompromising in his resentment of any form of falsehood or deceit. It was the force of his resentment in such a case that cost him his life."

Parkman had loaned $2,432 to Webster over the years and by 1849 he had run out of patience awaiting payment.

"Webster's careless financial habits were anathema to Parkman's parsimonious standards," according to "Murder at Harvard" on PBS's American Experience site.

Webster later admitted debt was his "downfall." Webster said after the trial that he had sent a note to Parkman asking for a meeting at the Medical School.

"It was to ask Dr. Parkman to call at my rooms on Friday the 23rd, after my lecture," Webster wrote. "He had become of late very importunate for his pay. He threatened me with a suit, to put an officer into my house, and to drive me from my professorship, if I did not pay him. The purport of my note was simply to ask the conference. . . . I wished to gain, for those few days, a release from his solicitations, to which I was liable every day on occasions and in a manner very disagreeable and alarming to me, and also to avert, for so long a time at least, the fulfillment of recent threats of severe measures."

On the morning of November 23, 1849, Webster went to Parkman's Beacon Hill residence to confirm that afternoon's meeting. About 2 p.m., Parkman was seen entering the Medical School, near the Charles River and a short walk from his home. He was never seen alive again.

"The doctor was unfailingly punctual in taking his meals," Irving wrote. "But on Friday, November 23, 1849, to his [wife and children's] surprise, Dr. Parkman did not come home to dinner; and their anxiety was increased when the day passed, and there was still no sign of the doctor's return."

Friends were immediately alarmed—it was so unlike Parkman—and the next day posters offering a $3,000 reward for help in locating Parkman alive were hung around the city. (The posters were later amended to a $1,000 reward for the body.) The Charles

River was dredged and by Sunday speculation on how and why Parkman disappeared consumed all classes in Boston. In the meantime, the Medical School's janitor, Ephraim Littlefield, had become suspicious of Webster. Late on that fateful Friday afternoon, Littlefield had found Webster's rooms locked from the inside, and heard water running. Webster left by a side door at 6:00 that evening and attended a bash at the house of friends that night; he was, as usual, the life of the party.

"His countenance was genial, his manner mild and unassuming; he was clean shaven, wore spectacles, and looked younger than his years," Irving wrote. "Professor Webster was popular with a large circle of friends. To those who liked him he was a man of pleasing and attractive manners, artistic in his tastes— he was especially fond of music—not a very profound or remarkable chemist, but a pleasant social companion. His temper was hasty and irritable. Spoilt in his boyhood as an only child, he was self-willed and self-indulgent. His wife and daughters were better liked than he. By unfriendly critics the Professor was thought to be selfish, fonder of the good things of the table and a good cigar than was consistent with his duty to his family or the smallness of his income."

On Saturday, Littlefield, who lived in the basement of the school with his wife, saw Webster with a bundle and Webster asked him to make a fire in the lab. On Sunday, Webster visited Parkman's family and told them he had paid Parkman the money he owed him on Friday, but that the meeting was brief and he had not seen the missing man since. By Tuesday, November 27, Parkman was still missing and his family and friends were panicking. Police searched Webster's rooms at the Medical School but found nothing. His private privy door was locked. On Wednesday, Littlefield's suspicions increased and he spied on Webster.

"Littlefield had watched under a door, seeing Webster's feet as far up as his knees, as the professor moved from the furnace to the fuel closet and back," Katherine Ramsland wrote in "George Parkman" in the Crime Library at Trutv.com. "He made eight separate trips, and later in the day, his furnace was burning so hard that the wall on the other side was hot to the touch."

On Thanksgiving, Littlefield, with his wife standing watch, began chiseling away at the brick wall under Webster's privy. He continued the next day.

"He went down a tunnel into the vault where the wall had felt so hot and began to hack at it right where Webster's lab privy emptied into a pit," Ramsland wrote. "He worked for quite some time until he managed to punch a hole into the wall, at which point he felt a draft so strong he could not get a lantern to stay lit inside. Maneuvering the lantern, he looked here and there, ignoring the foul fumes and letting his eyes adjust to the dark. Finally he saw something that seemed out of place. He narrowed his eyes and looked more sharply until he just made out on top of a dirt mound

$3,000 REWARD!

DR. GEORGE PARKMAN,

A well known citizen of Boston, left his residence No. 8 Walnut Street, on Friday last, he is 60 years of age ;—about 5 feet 9 inches high—grey hair—thin face— with a scar under his chin—light complexion—and usually walks very fast. He was dressed in a dark frock coat, dark pantaloons, purple silk vest, with dark figured black stock and black hat.

As he may have wandered from home in consequence of some sudden aberration of mind, being perfectly well when he left his house; or, as he had with him a large sum of money, he may have been foully dealt with. The above reward will be paid for information which will lead to his discovery if alive; or for the detection and conviction of the perpetrators if any injury may have been done to him.

A suitable reward will be paid for the discovery of his body.

Boston, Nov. 26th, 1849. **ROBERT G. SHAW.**

Information may be given to the City Marshal.

From the Congress Printing House,(Farwell & Co.) 32 Congress St.

This notice was posted around Boston after Parkman's disappearance.

the shape of a human pelvis. He also saw a dismembered thigh and the lower part of a leg."

Littlefield reported his discovery to police. The police picked Webster up at his home in Cambridge. They later discovered a partially burned torso with a thigh stuffed inside it in a tin case, and a bloodstained saw, in Webster's lab.

The Brahmins were doubly shocked, not only by the grotesque murder, but by the arrest of one of their own. Fanny Longfellow immediately pointed her finger at Littlefield, who had allegedly been supplementing his income by stealing bodies from graves and then selling them to medical students for $25.

"You will see by the papers what dark horror overshadows us like an eclipse," Fanny Longfellow wrote. "Of course we cannot believe Dr. Webster guilty, bad as the evidence looks. . . . Many suspect the janitor, who is known to be a bad man and to have wished for the reward offered for Dr. Parkman's body. He could make things appear against the doctor, having bodies under his control. I trust our minds will be soon relieved, but, meanwhile, they are soiled by new details continually. I went to see poor Mrs. Webster on Saturday, the day after her husband's arrest, but of course was not admitted. What a terrible blight upon her life and that of the girls! The mere suspicion, for I cannot believe anything can be proved."

Harvard librarian John Langdon Sibley concurred. He wrote in his journal that the university community was made distraught by the accusations—"the excitement, the melancholy, the aghastness of every body are indescribable. The professors poh! at the mere suspicion he is guilty. . . . People cannot eat; they feel sick."

Thousands of Bostonians lined the streets to watch Parkman's funeral procession on December 6, and thousands more took a tour of the Medical School to see where the murder had occurred. Webster initially had a problem finding a lawyer—the famous Daniel Webster, no relation, declined to take the case. The prosecution also had problems—how could they prove the parts that remained were from Parkman's body? A Grand Jury found probable cause that the body parts were Parkman's and that John Webster had killed him, but it still needed to be proven in a trial.

The trial began on March 19, 1850, and lasted twelve days. The near constant movement of spectators—sixty thousand people saw at least part of the proceedings—made the courtroom noisy, as did the frequent shouts for silence. Jury selection only took one hour; sixty-one men were questioned if they had formed an opinion of Webster's guilt and twelve who said they had not were empanelled in the jury box.

Attorney General John Clifford presented the prosecution's opening statement and talked for three hours about the facts of the case and a review of the evidence that would be presented. He conceded the body parts would not be recognizable. The next day, the jury visited the Medical School and even went down to the privy pit to see where the remains had been found.

Webster's defense team concentrated on establishing doubt that anyone could actually identify these remains as those of George Parkman—after all, they were discovered in a medical school where bodies were often dissected. The key to the prosecution's case turned out to be Dr. Nathan Keep, Parkman's dentist, who said unequivocally that the false teeth in the jawbone found in the furnace were the ones he had made for George Parkman in 1846. The plaster cast for the dentures was introduced as evidence. When Keep demonstrated how the loose teeth found in the furnace also fit his plates, he burst into tears. Ironically, Parkman had ordered the dentures because of the opening of the Medical School.

"In anticipation of being asked to make a speech on this occasion Dr. Parkman, whose teeth were few and far between, had himself fitted by Dr. Keep with a complete set of false teeth," Irving wrote. "Oliver Wendell Holmes . . . who was present at the opening of the college noticed how very nice and white the doctor's teeth appeared to be. It was the discovery of the remains of these same admirable teeth three years later in the furnace in Professor Webster's lower laboratory that led to the conviction of Dr. Parkman's murderer. By a strange coincidence the doctor met his death in the very college which his generosity had helped to build."

Littlefield was the prosecution's star witness. His wife also testified. Both were unshakable, even when the defense attorneys suggested that Littlefield was out to get the reward. "I never have made or intend to make any claim for either of the rewards that have been offered," he replied. (He did accept $3,000 as a gift from Parkman's family afterward.)

"Littlefield made a strong impression on the jury," Ramsland wrote. "He was confident and seemed honest, and there was nothing the defense could do to break down his story. What they did not do, although Webster had suggested it . . . was to accuse Littlefield himself of doing the deed."

Webster decided to take the stand but his testimony had little effect. When Judge Shaw charged the jury, he had to address the fact that no identifiable body, corpus delicti, had been produced. His pronouncement that "reasonable certainty" was enough to convict became a standard of American justice.

The jury members quickly agreed that the body was Parkman's and that John Webster had killed him. After some discussion, they also voted that the slaying had been a "willful act," meaning the death penalty would be automatic. "The verdict of guilty was reached by the jury after a couple of hours of prayer and a few minutes of deliberation," Levy wrote in *The Law of the Commonwealth and Chief Justice Shaw*. "Yet the case stands, according to an authority, 'as a classic example of how a jury can reach a sound verdict despite an unfair trial.'"

Webster was visibly stunned when the foreman pronounced "Guilty." He "started like a person shot," according to one trial report. "His hand dropped to the rail in front, his chin drooped down upon his breast, and after remaining thus a moment, he sank into the chair, covering his eyes with his hands. A deathlike silence followed, and all eyes were fixed in sadness on him whose hopes had now fled." Two days later, Shaw, citing the law, "every person who shall commit the crime of murder shall suffer the punishment of death for the same," sentenced Webster to "be hung by the neck until you are dead. May God, in his infinite goodness, have mercy on your soul." His lawyers unsuccessfully sought to overturn the verdict by submitting a writ of error against Judge Shaw for the argumentative way he had charged the jury, claiming that he had implied "malice aforethought" was a given. From his jail cell, Webster appealed to Governor George Briggs for a pardon but that was also denied.

In a last-ditch effort to avoid death, Webster narrated a 3,286-word confession in jail to the Reverend George Putnam, admitting to the gruesome murder. He also apologized to the Parkman family, and for casting aspersions on the Littlefields. His hope was that by admitting to the murder, but denying it was premeditated, he would win a reprieve from the gallows. He said he had arranged to meet Parkman at the Medical School on the fateful day to ask him for more time.

"He would not listen to me, but interrupted me with much vehemence," Webster wrote. "He called me 'scoundrel' and 'liar,' and went on heaping upon me the most bitter taunts and opprobrious epithets. While he was talking, he drew . . . an old letter from Dr. Hosack, written many years ago, and congratulating him (Dr. P.) on his success in getting me appointed professor of chemistry. 'You see,' he said, 'I got you into your office, and now I will get you out of it.' He put back into his pocket all of the papers, except the letter and the notes. I cannot tell how long the torrent of threats and invectives continued, and I can now recall to memory but a small portion of what he said. At first I kept interposing, trying to pacify him, so that I might obtain the object for which I had sought the interview. But I could not stop him, and soon my own temper was up. I forgot everything. I felt nothing but the sting of his words. I was excited to the highest degree of passion; and while he was speaking and gesticulating in the most violent and menacing manner, thrusting the letter and his fist into my face, in my fury I seized whatever thing was handiest,—it was a stick of wood,—and dealt him an instantaneous blow with all the force that passion could give it. I did not know, nor think, nor care where I should hit him, nor how hard, nor to what the effort would be. It was on the side of his head, and there was nothing to break the force of the blow. He fell instantly upon the pavement. There was no second blow. He did not move. I stooped down over him, and he seemed to be lifeless. Blood flowed from his mouth, and I got a sponge and wiped it away. I got some ammonia and applied it to his nose; but without effect. Perhaps I spent ten minutes in attempts to resuscitate him; but I found that he was absolutely dead. In my horror and consternation I ran instinctively to the doors and bolted them—the doors of the lecture room, and the laboratory below. And then, what was I to do? It never occurred to me to go out and declare what had been done, and obtain assistance. I saw nothing but the alternative of a successful removal and concealment of the body, on the one hand, and of infamy and destruction on the other."

On August 30, 1850, after visiting with his wife and daughters in his jail cell, John W. Webster was marched to the gallows in Leverett Square and publicly hanged. He died within four minutes and was interred at Copp's Hill Burying Ground. George Parkman's widow later generously donated to a fund established for the welfare of Mrs. Webster and her daughters.

CHAPTER 5

A. Bronson Alcott
"For physical toil he had no affinity"

A. Bronson Alcott was a great thinker.
A great worker? Not so much.

"Somebody once described 'Fruitlands' as a place where Mr. Alcott looked benign and talked philosophy while Mrs. Alcott and the children did the work," recalled Isaac Hecker, a participant in Alcott's famed 1843 utopian experiment. "Still to look benign is a good deal for a man to do persistently in an adverse world . . . and Mr. Alcott persevered in that exercise until his latest day."

Fruitlands lasted for only seven months in Harvard, a small Massachusetts town thirty miles west of Boston. Hecker, who later became a Roman Catholic priest and founder of the Paulist Fathers, bailed in less than two months. He gave five reasons for leaving, two of which were: "the fact that [Alcott's] place has very little fruit on it, when it was and is their desire that fruit should be the principal part of their diet" and "my fear that they have a too decided tendency toward literature and writing for the prosperity and success of their enterprise."

It may be somewhat unfair to call Alcott a jerk, although the press and many others did during his lifetime. One popular definition of Alcott and his fellow Transcendentalists at the time was that they "dove into the infinite, soared into the illimitable, and never paid cash." Alcott, though, was centuries ahead of his time in his philosophy of education. He was also an unapologetic abolitionist who walked the walk and lost his precious Temple School in Boston for, among other reasons, refusing to expel a black girl he had enrolled. But in some ways, he certainly was an arrogant jerk. Those who joined him at Fruitlands often found him "despotic." His wife Abby and daughters adored him, but his inability to adapt and make a living caused them to move more than twenty times in thirty years, and his physical laziness caused them to work their fingers to the bone. Still, they remained devoted to him, and Abby Alcott, whom he married in 1830, once wrote a friend that she feared he was going insane because of his failures.

His great friend, Ralph Waldo Emerson, while praising Alcott's intellect, couldn't resist taking a shot at his inability to turn his ideas into a living.

"Alcott," Emerson wrote, "is an intellectual Torso,—he has vision without any talent,—a colossal head and trunk without hands or feet; and I think we must say of him what Lessing said in Emilia Galeotti: 'Do you suppose, Prince, that Raffaelle would not have been the greatest genius among painters, even though unfortunately he should have been born without hands?'"

The torso—and the rest of Alcott—was born on Spindle Hill, Wolcott, Connecticut, on November 29, 1799. His parents, Anna Bronson and Joseph Chatfield Alcock, named him Amos Bronson. He was called Amos until he was twenty when he made his first name just the initial A. and changed his last name. (According to Jan Freeman in the *Boston Globe:* "Our rooster and weather vane date from the 19th century, when cock became too vivid for polite American discourse. So strong was the taboo that Bronson Alcock, father of Louisa May, changed the family name to Alcott.")

Bronson's great-grandfather, John Alcock, had settled Spindle Hill in 1731. John Alcock acquired more than a thousand acres, which he later passed on to his eleven children—including Bronson's patriarchal grandfather, also John, who fought in the Revolutionary War. Spindle Hill was all Alcocks when Bronson was growing up. Bronson's father Joseph was illiterate, but a good flax farmer and fine toolmaker.

Like his mother, young Bronson was tall, fair, and blue-eyed. With her encouragement, he taught himself to read and write by forming letters in charcoal on the kitchen floorboards. After reading John Bunyan's book, *Pilgrim's Progress,* Bronson left home at the age of seventeen to become a peddler in Virginia and the

A. BRONSON ALCOTT AT THE AGE OF 53

From the portrait by Mrs. Hildreth

A. Bronson Alcott

Carolinas. When he was twenty-two, he returned to Connecticut —$400 in debt—and decided to become a teacher. Education became his lifelong passion. He was drawn to Swiss educator Johann Pestalozzi's philosophy that children are basically good and that every aspect of a child's life contributes to the formation of personality, character, and reason. Pestalozzi's educational philosophy would heavily influence America's soon-to-blossom Transcendentalism movement, with Alcott one of its foremost champions. The New England writers and thinkers who espoused Transcendentalism beginning in the 1830s based their beliefs on the work of eighteenth-century German philosopher Immanuel Kant. The Transcendentalists believed people are born good, and that through intuition and observing nature they can become closer to God.

While other schools would beat the three Rs into children, Alcott's schools in Pennsylvania, Connecticut, and Massachusetts introduced art, music, nature study, field trips, recess, and physical education into the curriculum. Alcott did not use or allow corporal punishment. He preferred the Socratic Method and encouraged his students to ask questions.

"My father taught in the wise way which unfolds what lies in the child's nature, as a flower blooms, rather than crammed it, like a Strasbourg goose, with more than it could digest," Louisa May Alcott later wrote.

Many parents did not appreciate Alcott's radical methods— around that same time his future friend Henry David Thoreau was fired from a Concord school because he refused to beat his students. Alcott's schools invariably failed, thus the twenty moves in thirty years. The hardships fell on his wife Abigail, the descendent of a prominent Boston family, whose reform instincts and intellect matched Alcott's. Together, they had four daughters and a son who died soon after he was born. Their youngest daughter, May, grew up to be a critically acclaimed artist. Louisa, their second daughter, became a renowned writer (*Little Women*), and her royalties wound up supporting the family since dear old dad couldn't.

In 1834 Alcott embarked on his most famous and controversial educational experiment with the opening of the Temple School on Fremont Street in Boston. He enrolled thirty boys and girls who ranged in age from six to twelve years old. He hired fellow Transcendentalists Elizabeth Palmer Peabody and Margaret Fuller as assistants. Much of the teaching was based on conversations about the New Testament, some of which Alcott transcribed in his publication *Conversations with Children on the Gospels* in 1836 and 1837.

Conversations proved to be controversial, as did Alcott's other progressive methods. The *Courier,* a Boston newspaper, quoted an anonymous clergyman who called Alcott's teaching method "one-third absurd, one-third blasphemous, and one-third obscene." Alcott was jeered in the streets, and parents began pulling their children out of the Temple School. The Panic of 1837—what we now would call a depression—also caused enrollment to drop. After Alcott accepted a black girl into his school in 1838, even his abolitionist supporters balked and he was left with just five students—three of his daughters, the black girl, and one boy. He closed the school in 1839 and for a time lived off of handouts from friends and income from a series of conversations he held in people's parlors. Alcott also helped start the Transcendentalists' *The Dial* magazine and contributed his much-ballyhooed "Orphic Sayings."

"Listen divinely to the sibyl within thee, saith the Spirit, and write thou her words. For now is thine intellect a worshipper of the Holy Ghost; now thy life is mystic—thy words marvels—and thine appeal to the total sense of man—a nature to the soul," is an example of one.

Working-class newspaper readers, Ivy League academics, and even some supporters of Alcott and the Transcendentalists found the 112 sayings published between 1840 and 1842 pompous and a little hard to take. "Who reads *The Dial* for any other purpose than to laugh at its baby poetry or at the solemn fooleries of its misty prose?" one Yale intellectual wrote. The *Boston Transcript* parodied Bronson's efforts under the title "Gastric Sayings," while a letter to the *Boston Post* compared the sayings to "a train of fif-teen railroad cars with one passenger." Octavius Brooks Froth-ingham, an unapologetic supporter of the Transcendentalists, admitted these sayings "were an amazement to the uninitiated and an amusement to the profane." (As late as 2005, a critic in the *Christian Science Monitor* wrote the "Orphic Sayings," "read like a collection of stale fortune cookies at a New Age restaurant.")

Others, however, insisted they were works of great accom-plishment, comparable to Benjamin Franklin's or Emerson's apho-risms.

"In his 'Orphic Sayings' Mr. Alcott presented, as we have seen, the Neo-Platonist view of the world, and thus gave to his contem-poraries the shock which they needed," F. B. Sanborn and William T. Harris wrote in their 1893 book, *A. Bronson Alcott, His Life and Philosophy*. "This is evident by the uproar of ridicule and indigna-tion which ensued. American common-sense and Fourth-of-July democracy had never considered the possibility of any other view of the world than its own. . . . Alcott's contributions [to *The Dial*], particularly the 'Orphic Sayings,' were the occasion of boundless ridicule in the *Boston Post* and in Beacon Street drawing rooms. . . . Great was the laughter in Boston, and lively, no doubt, the village cachinnation of Concord, when the *Boston Post* daily burlesqued Alcott in *The Dial* and Emerson in his lecture room . . . with more copious rhetoric, specially barbed for Alcott and Emerson, recited this: —'With uncouth words they tire their tender lungs, The same bald phrases on their hundred tongues: 'Ever' 'The Ages' in their page appear, 'Always' the bedlamite is called a 'Seer.'"

Despite the criticism and opposition, Alcott remained con-vinced he could improve "the perishable and shameful civilization of America," according to Sanborn and Wells.

"That this hostility and misconception of his real purpose (which was high and beneficent) did not drive our philosopher into bitterness or insanity, is one of the surest evidences of his intel-lectual greatness," his fawning biographers wrote. "He continued to love mankind when they rejected him."

The butt of jokes to many in America—even Emerson noted Alcott's spiritual spiels "always end with 'give us much land and money'"—the consummate sponger found allies in England, particularly the eccentric and wealthy Charles Lane. "Prosaic, sincere and courageous in living up to the articles of his faith, Lane was ready to be victimized by any project which promised to realize his dream of a 'True Harmonic Association,'" Lindsay Swift wrote in *Brook Farm: Its Members, Scholars, and Visitors,* published in 1900. "An opportunity for complete disaster soon came and was embraced."

Alcott and Lane became convinced that the Transcendentalist ideal—a utopian society—remained possible. Several experiments were already underway; the best known one attempted in Massachusetts was the two-hundred-acre Brook Farm in West Roxbury, where George Ripley, a former Unitarian minister and later a literary critic for the *New York Tribune,* attempted to put the plain living theories of Emerson into practice from 1841 to 1847. Brook Farm had about one hundred members, including intellectuals, carpenters, farmers, shoemakers, and printers. Everyone worked up to ten hours each day, whether in farming or other industries. A fire in 1846, followed by a lawsuit filed by writer Nathaniel Hawthorne to reclaim his investment, spelled the end of Brook Farm.

Alcott and Lane visited Brook Farm, as well as a Shaker community in the hills of Harvard, before Lane purchased a stunning ninety-acre parcel near the Shaker tract for $1,800. The two men named it Fruitlands because they intended to live off the fruits of the land.

"Why, then, did [Alcott] not go with Ripley?" wrote Swift. "There is no sure answer, but we may, in fairness, suppose that he would have stayed long away from a project which involved 300 days' labor in each year, with an average of 54 working hours to each week of six days. This philosopher would gladly have conversed under a noonday sun until the sweat poured down his face, but for physical toil he had no affinity. The nebular state of most projects was definite enough for Mr. Alcott."

If you thought you knew Fruitlands...

In the late spring of 1843, Alcott, Abby, their four daughters, and Lane and his son moved to the Fruitlands commune. Eight other adults—most of questionable rationality—soon arrived. The "Con-Sociates" included Samuel Larned from Rhode Island, who rebelled against the status quo by swearing at everyone he met. Joe Palmer had been persecuted and jailed for wearing a beard at a time when no one else did. Hecker was a baker and spiritual searcher. Abram Wood was a cooper who had previously been in an insane asylum; he insisted on being called Wood Abram. There was also a nudist. The only adult woman in the group besides Abby Alcott, Ann Page, was soon expelled for eating a piece of fish.

Alcott and Lane—"bottomless imbeciles" according to their contemporary Thomas Carlyle—believed all contact with social institutions corrupted man's innate goodness. They considered commerce and the desire for material goods to be demeaning. They saw industrial work as particularly bad for the soul. The Con-Sociates became the strictest of vegetarians—they wouldn't even use honey because it belonged to the bees or milk because it belonged to cows. Alcott ordered that no one kill the canker worms that infested the fruit trees because "they had as much right to the apples as man did." Alcott's and Lane's plan for Fruitlands was that the members would work by day in the fields—unfertilized because Alcott thought manure was "filth"—and discuss philosophy at night.

"Here we prosecute our efforts to initiate a Family in harmony with the primitive instincts of man," Lane and Alcott wrote in a joint letter to *The Dial* on June 10, 1843. "Ordinary secular farming" was not in the program, they said. They planned to supersede the "labor of the plough and cattle by the spade and pruning knife." They put their faith in the "succors of an ever bounteous Providence" and in "uncorrupted fields and unworldly persons."

Alcott and Lane didn't even think it right to use oxen or mules to pull plows. The philosophers decided to "rely wholly on the spade instead of the plough," even at a cost of valuable time, according to historian Clara Endicott Sears. "The results were rather disastrous: Charles Lane's hands became sore and painful, and lame backs seriously interfered with progress." Palmer, the only Con-Sociate with any farming experience, is credited with keeping the experiment going for as long as it lasted—for starters he went home to No Town (now part of Leominster) shortly after his arrival and returned with a cow and ox yoked together to pull a plow.

Emerson visited in early July and then wrote in his journal, "They look well in July; we will see them in December." Emerson couldn't help but note, though, that little work was being done. "All day, all night, they hold perpetual parliament."

Most bailed out well before December. Historian Sears, who would later purchase Fruitlands and turn it into the museum it is today, noted in her 1915 book *Bronson Alcott's Fruitlands* that Alcott and Lane didn't even know where to plant trees.

"The philosophers had planted three mulberry trees next to the front door, and they had set out apple trees and pear trees below the house on the slope of the hill," Sears wrote. "They put the mulberry trees so near the house that when they grew, the roots almost unsettled the foundations, and the fruit trees were planted in just the wrong place to permit of luxuriant growth; but they never knew it, and at the time they pictured to themselves the full-grown trees with branches overladen with the luscious ripening fruit."

The Fruitlands experiment started to fall apart as the Con-Sociates began bickering. The work began to fall more and more on Abby Alcott and her two oldest daughters, twelve-year-old Anna and ten-year-old Louisa. When a visitor asked Abby Alcott if the commune had any beasts of burden she replied sarcastically, "Only one woman." In her diary, she seemed a bit less amused about her husband and Lane, remarking that "they spare the cattle, but they forget the women and children." When Bronson Alcott and Lane left in the fall to unsuccessfully try to recruit new members—and Palmer returned to No Town to harvest his own crop there—Abby Alcott and her children were the only ones left to bring in the meager barley harvest.

"What is to be our destiny I can in no wise guess," Lane wrote to a friend. "Mr. Alcott makes such high requirements of all persons that few are likely to stay, even of his own family, unless he can become more tolerant of defect."

Despite the inescapable failure of Fruitlands, Alcott remained pompous. "Great is the man," he wrote, "whom his age despises, for transcendent excellence is purchased through the obloquy of contemporaries; and shame is the gate of the temple of renown." Richard Francis, author of *Fruitlands: The Alcott Family and Their Search for Utopia,* noted that Alcott's "capacity for not being ironic seems almost infinite." Sears related this story about the trip in search of recruits: "On their return from New York they went by steamer to New Haven. All the money that had been contributed by . . . friends had gone, but that did not trouble the philosophers. They boarded the boat quite serenely and when it started sat on deck enjoying the breeze. The ticket-man came to each passenger for his ticket, and when he came to Mr. Alcott and Mr. Lane, sitting there in their linen suits, he asked them for theirs. Quite undisturbed Mr. Alcott replied that they had no money or scrip, but they would quite willingly pay their way by addressing the passengers and crew with a little conversation in the saloon. It is said that in reply the language of the ticket-man was not as civil as it should have been."

The Fruitlands experiment lasted just seven months. Without sufficient food supplies or firewood, the Alcotts—with deeply depressed Bronson the last to leave—returned to Concord in January 1844. Preacher William Ellery Channing later said Abby Alcott wrote him that Bronson became so depressed she thought he was going insane: "He did such strange things without seeming to know how odd they were; wearing only linen clothes and canvas shoes, and eating only vegetables."

Once Alcott overcame his depression, he began leading his "Conversations" again, although participants were often disappointed at their lack of direction. "All the beauty and advantages of Conversation is in its bold contrasts, and swift surprises," he responded. "Prose and logic are out of place, where all is flowing, magical, and free." His detractors found his pomposity aggravating and thought he might have been "tapping the spring of his friend's genius." Judge E. R. Hoar of Concord observed, "What is the difference between Emerson and Alcott? One is a seer; the other a seer sucker."

In his later years, Alcott traveled throughout the Midwest on lecture tours and during the Civil War he served as Superintendent of Schools in Concord. In 1879 with financial backing from friends, he founded the Concord School of Philosophy. The school continued until July 1888, four months after he died on March 4. Daughter Louisa May died two days later of mercury poisoning.

"Alcott was for many years, between 1837 and 1870, and even during the later period of the Concord School of Philosophy, the target for much cheap wit and for some censure, as a person who might have many kinds of sense but had not common-sense," Wells and Sanborn wrote. "Few persons would seem to have been so completely outside of their proper time and place as Alcott."

CHAPTER 6

Joshua V. Himes
Press Secretary for the Great Disappointment *Millerism*

As founder and pastor of the Chardon Street Chapel in Boston, the Reverend Joshua Vaughan Himes had made quite a name for himself as a progressive reformer before he was even thirty-five years old.

Himes was a natural promoter and during the 1830s his church became the reform headquarters of Boston, home to temperance, women's rights, and pacifist organizations, and the birthplace of William Lloyd Garrison's New England Anti-Slavery Society.

Imagine Garrison's disappointment in 1840 when Himes told him that he and his wife would be curtailing all reform activities, including the sacred campaign of abolition, to devote themselves to an even greater—as in End of the World greater—cause.

In November 1839, Himes had met William Miller in Exeter, New Hampshire, and invited him to speak at the five-hundred-seat Chardon Street Chapel. Miller was a country preacher, a well-meaning rube from western Massachusetts who had been beating the rural bushes of northern New England, upstate New York, and southern Ontario for eight years, preaching that the return of Jesus and the destruction of Earth by fire would take place between March 21, 1843, and March 21, 1844.

Miller came to the Hub in December. He stayed at Himes's home and soon wrote to his son: "I am now in this place lecturing twice a day to large audiences —many, very many, go away unable to gain admittance. Many, I am informed, are under serious convictions. I hope God will work in this city."

Himes was one of those "under serious convictions." In fact, Miller's apocalyptical preaching blew Himes away. Himes asked

Miller if he would be interested in getting his message out to far more people and in other urban areas. Miller said yes.

"I then told him he might prepare for the campaign, for doors should be opened in every city in the Union, and the warning should go to the ends of the earth!" Himes later wrote. "Here I began to help Father Miller."

What ensued was a media blitz of historic proportions engineered by Himes. Miller had the message—and Himes had the savvy to get that message out. Soon Millerism would sweep the eastern part of the country, especially the Northeast. With Himes as media director, Miller's Adventist message even reached England, Scotland, and Ireland.

"Himes proved a godsend to Miller," Paul Conklin wrote in his book, *American Originals: Homemade Varieties of Christianity.* "He had a broad network of friends and, most critical, exceptional editorial and publishing skills."

On March 20, 1840, Himes published the initial *Signs of the Times* newspaper—the first of many millions of printed pieces he would publish for the cause. He also planned and promoted lecture tours for Miller outside rural New England, including in New York City. Himes soon was publishing several other newspapers, too— *Advent Witness, Voice of Warning, Trumpet of Alarm, Glad Tidings of the Kingdom to Come,* and the *Midnight Cry* in New York City. He also pumped out pamphlets, charts, hymn books, and copies of Miller's lectures. They all had one message—repent, the end is at hand. The words of "Father Miller" and other Millerite preachers who fanned out as far as Ohio and Washington, DC—at least twenty of whom were female—whipped people into a frenzy.

"The Reverend Joshua V. Himes, a man of indomitable energy . . . took Prophet Miller out from the simple, peaceful, rural districts and placed him in the lime-light of city thoroughfares, there to sound his note of warning above the din of countless noises and the clamor of innumerable voices," Clara Endicott Sears wrote in

1924 in her *Days of Delusion*. "It will be seen how this change was like sowing the wind and reaping the whirlwind as regards the simple-minded old prophet, who was fast aging under the stress of the situation he had created, and that now threatened to overwhelm him."

Himes knew controversy sells papers—he even included many letters critical of Miller in *Signs of the Times* in a section called "Refuge of Scoffers." The circulation and the hysteria rose at a fever pitch until October 22, 1844, a day that became forevermore known as "The Great Disappointment."

Though partners in promoting the apocalypse, Himes and Miller were as different as two people could be.

Miller was sixty years old in 1842, rumpled and running out of energy. He had been born in Pittsfield, the oldest of sixteen children, but grew up a poor country boy in rural Vermont and upstate New York.

Himes turned thirty-seven in 1842. He was full of energy, always well dressed, and had lived in cities his entire life. A natural huckster, he's been compared to P. T. Barnum in his ability to promote. He was born on May 19, 1805, in North Kingstown, Rhode Island. His wealthy father was a West India trader and a prominent member of the Episcopal Church. The family planned for young Joshua to attend Brown University and become an Episcopalian preacher, but in 1817, one of the ship captains who sailed for the elder Himes stole a ship and its cargo and plunged the Himes family into destitution. College was out, so Joshua was sent to New Bedford, Massachusetts, to become a cabinetmaker's apprentice. At eighteen, he joined the Christian Church in New Bedford and four years later became the pastor of a church in Fall River. In 1830 just twenty-five years old, he became pastor of the First Christian Church in Boston. His progressive social ideas rankled some, though, and the congregation split in two. The fifty members who aligned with Himes elected him as pastor of the Second Christian Church. Soon their number grew to five hundred and Chardon Street Chapel was built.

The Chardon Street Chapel quickly became the home for reformers in Boston. Suffragists, pacifists, abolitionists, and temperance supporters all met there. More, however, was afoot than reform in Boston and the nation in the late 1830s. Religious revivals and pseudosciences such as phrenology (the belief that the contours of a man's skull revealed his character) were sweeping the land. A cholera epidemic, a sensational meteor shower on November 13, 1833, and memories of the blotting out of the sun in New England one day in 1780—known later to have been caused by huge forest fires in the untamed West—were seen as signs by many that the end of the world was surely near. The economic growth of the 1820s and 1830s also came to an abrupt end, with the Panic of 1837 ushering in a depression. Meanwhile, more and more Catholics, whom many Protestants reviled as a menace (Millerites even considered the Pope the anti-Christ), were coming to America through the ports of Boston and New York.

The time was ripe for doomsday predictions. But while others cried, "the end is coming," Miller actually set a date—the year between March 21, 1843, and March 21, 1844—when Jesus would return and "purify the earth by fire causing the wicked and all their works to be consumed in the general conflagration."

Miller had not arrived at the date whimsically. He only had eighteen months of schooling as a child, but he was a voracious reader, and while living in Poultney, Vermont, he was a farmer, sheriff, justice of the peace, and a respected community leader. In 1803 he became a deist—one who believes God created the world but has little interest in what happened after that. Then Miller served as an infantry captain in the War of 1812.

"A fatal blow to Miller's deistic outlook was delivered at the battle of Plattsburgh, where he and only about 5,000 other Americans squared off against a reported 15,000 British troops," Richard Abanes wrote in his 1998 book, *End-Time Visions: The Road to Armageddon?.* "Miller believed that they would experience a devastating defeat unless God intervened. After several grueling skirmishes on both land and sea, the American forces scored a decisive victory over the British fleet on September 11, 1814. It was a battle in which Miller had played a 'courageous part.' Plattsburgh ultimately spelled disaster not only for the king's invading units, but also for Miller's flagging deism. God, it seemed to Miller, had actually stepped into time and space to perform a miracle."

After the war, Miller moved his family to a two-hundred-acre farm in Low Hampton, New York, just across the Vermont border. He was plagued by the bloody, apocalyptical horrors he witnessed at Plattsburgh and began to question his own beliefs about life and death, good and evil. "I was truly wretched," he later wrote, "but did not understand the cause . . . . I mourned, but without hope."

Miller, often described as a "kind and good man" who helped slaves escape to Canada on the Underground Railroad, rejoined his uncle's Baptist church and started studying the Bible. In 1816—known as the Year of No Summer because there was a frost in New England every month—Miller began an intense examination of Scripture. Two years later, cherry-picking from the Old Testament and using a complicated mathematical formula, he concluded "in about twenty-five years from that time all the affairs of our present state would be wound up." He later wrote, "I am fully convinced that sometime between March 21st, 1843, and March 21st, 1844 . . . Christ will come and bring all his saints with him."

For a decade, Miller shared his conclusion only with close friends, but in 1831 he decided—after hearing a voice that said "Go, and tell it to the world"—that it was his duty to warn others. The following year, he published his ideas serially in the *Vermont Telegraph*. In 1833 he published a pamphlet and hit the lecture circuit to spread his vision, warning rural congregations throughout the Northeast to prepare for the imminent return of Christ.

"You, O impenitent men and women, where will you be then?" Miller would ask in his sermons. "When heaven shall resound with the mighty song, and distant realms shall echo back the sound, where, tell me where, will you be then? In hell! O think! In hell! . . . lifting up your eyes, being in torment. Stop sinner, think! In hell.

Where the beast and the false prophet are, and shall be tormented day and night, forever and ever."

In his memoirs later published by Himes, Miller estimated that in the next dozen years he gave more than 4,500 lectures attended by at least 500,000 people. One of those people was Himes. Their meeting was a match made in apocalyptic heaven (or hell, as it turned out).

"A unique and effective fit took shape between millennialism and mass communication," David Morgan wrote in his 1999 book *Protestants & Pictures: Religion, Visual Culture and the Age of American Mass Production.* "The Millerites exploited the daily newspaper, the private mail, and the widely circulated, inexpensively produced pamphlets and periodicals . . . *The Midnight Cry* reported that six hundred thousand pieces of Adventist literature had been circulated in New York City in a single year. *The Voice of Truth* reported that by May 1844, five million Millerite periodicals had been put into circulation. One preacher boasted that by 1842, Adventist pamphlets, tracts, and books had been sent to 'every missionary station in Europe, Asia, Africa, America, and both sides of the Rocky Mountains.'"

The great thinkers of the day and associates of Himes in reform—Garrison, Bronson Alcott, Theodore Parker, James Russell Lowell, and Ralph Waldo Emerson—all attended Millerite meetings at Chardon Street Church, although none of them ended up joining. Tens of thousands of others did. Under Himes's direction, the Millerites built their own tabernacle in Boston in 1842 and camp meetings flourished, some under a tent that held more than four thousand people and was said to be the largest ever constructed. Miller, Himes, and other Millerite preachers attracted crowds with three-foot-by-six-foot charts depicting colorful, bizarre images of the Apocalypse—angels blowing trumpets, lions with wings, dragons with seven heads, grotesque beasts with bared teeth.

"In the age of P. T Barnum, Americans seemed to have a boundless appetite for spectacle and entertainment, and the tent turned out to be an inspired advertising ploy," Catherine A. Brekus wrote in her 1998 book *Strangers & Pilgrims: Female Preaching in America, 1740–1845.* "Barnum himself, the master of humbug, later imitated the Millerites by buying an enormous tent for his 'Greatest Show on Earth.' Whether or not Barnum ever attended a Millerite meeting, he knew expert salesmanship when he saw it. Many of his circus posters, with their pictures of ferocious-looking beasts, looked remarkably like the Millerites' prophetic charts."

In 1843 Millerism reached a fever pitch. The number of Millerites has been conservatively estimated at fifty thousand; some put the number at one hundred thousand or more. Pockets of Millerism sprang up in Canada and Great Britain. Publisher Horace Greeley in New York and other journalists in Boston and Philadelphia warned that Miller's doomsday prediction constituted a huge public threat. "If your preaching drives people into despair or insanity, you are responsible for the consequences," lexicographer Noah Webster wrote to Miller. A Philadelphia newspaper editorialized, "After some half-dozen more deaths occur and a few more men and women are sent to madhouses by this miserable fanaticism perhaps some grand jury may think it worthwhile to indict the vagabonds who are the cause of so much mischief."

As the March end date grew near, some men stopped working, some farmers stopped farming, businesses closed, and many Millerites gave all of their money and possessions to heirs and even strangers.

"On March 21, 1844, some of the more fanatical Millerites completely lost control," Abanes wrote. "A Boston journalist who had been following the story reported to the *New York Herald* that many Millerites had actually jumped from roofs and treetops in hopes of timing their leaps with Christ's return. But Jesus did not return and those who jumped 'were critically hurt, and some fell to their deaths.'"

After March 21 came—and went—the public and press had a field day and the Millerites were ridiculed. The headline of one

Boston newspaper read: "What!—not gone up yet?—We thought you'd gone up! Aren't you going up soon?—Wife didn't go up and leave you behind to burn, did she?"

Miller, in poor health for more than a year, was embarrassed and determined to figure out how he had miscalculated. He wrote Himes a letter about children ridiculing him on the streets. In another letter he wrote, "I confess my error, and acknowledge my disappointment [however] I still believe that the day of the Lord is near, even at the door."

Some of Miller's followers gave up, but most, including Himes, did not. Though desperate and hurt, they found solace in Miller's words that "soon our time, and all prophetic days, will have been filled." Numerous Christian, Methodist, and Free Will Baptist congregations divided over Miller's prediction. Excommunications, "disfellowships," and schisms occurred, and some Adventists established churches of their own.

In August, Millerite Samuel S. Snow's recalculation, called the "Seventh Month Message" (a reference to the seventh month in the Jewish calendar), set the end date as October 22. It took hold at a camp meeting in New Hampshire and quickly spread like wind-whipped hellfire through the Adventist churches.

Burned by the March prediction, neither Miller nor Himes endorsed the new date at first. But tens of thousands of Adventists, after so much doubt and embarrassment, seized on it "with great enthusiasm," according to Conklin.

"The date quickly became a self-fulfilling prophecy," Conklin wrote. "Its impact was so great and the fervor of the new revival so irresistible that Himes and Miller finally capitulated in early October, under conviction that the Holy Spirit had to be behind such wonderful effects."

On October 6 Miller wrote in the *Advent Herald,* "I see a glory in the seventh month which I never saw before. . . . I see a beauty, a harmony, and an agreement in the scriptures. . . . I am almost home, Glory! Glory!! Glory!! . . . . If he does not come within 20 or 25 days, I shall feel twice the disappointment I did this spring."

Himes was next. Adventist author Everett Dick wrote in 1938's *Founders of the Message,* "On October 9, Mr. Himes came out in favor of the new view, confessing his imperfection, pride of opinion and self, and his slowness to receive new truths when they came to him."

On October 12 Himes published what he expected to be the last edition of the *Advent Herald.* "We therefore find our work is now finished and that all we have to do is to go out to meet the Bridegroom and to trim our lamps accordingly. . . . Your blood be upon your own heads."

On October 22 the faithful made ready. Millerites in Salem marched in white ascension robes to Gallows Hill where Puritans had hanged witches 152 years earlier. Thousands gathered at the Millerite tabernacle in Boston. Some believers in Central Massachusetts scaled Mount Wachusett, while others climbed trees or simply waited in their homes. Throughout the Northeast, tens of thousands who followed Miller waited for the Second Coming of Christ, many donning robes and climbing hilltops or into trees to be closer to heaven. Some had given away their farms, homes, and all of their worldly possessions.

"Crops were left unharvested, their owners expecting never to want what they had raised," Luther Boutelle, a Millerite preacher from Groton, wrote in his memoirs. "Men paid up their debts. Many sold their property to help others to pay their debts. . . . Beef cattle were slaughtered and distributed among the poor."

October 22 came.

And October 22 went.

"We looked for our coming Lord until the clock tolled 12 at midnight," farmer Hiram Edson of Port Gibson, New York, wrote. "The day had then passed and our disappointment became a certainty. . . . We wept and wept till the day dawned."

Some Millerites committed suicide after the Great Disappointment, their embarrassment too much to bear.

"Still in the cold world," Boutelle wrote in his memoirs. "No deliverance—the Lord had not come. . . . It was a humiliating thing,

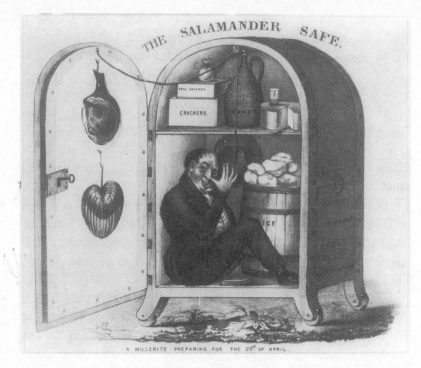

An 1843 cartoon by Thomas Sinclair mocking the Millerites

LIBRARY OF CONGRESS LC-USZ62-23784

and we all felt it alike." Joseph Bates, a friend of Miller's, wrote: "I had been a respected citizen, and had with much confidence exhorted the people to be ready for the expected change. . . . If the earth could have opened and swallowed me up, it would have been sweetness compared to the distress I felt."

Millerism was dead, buried in a sea of ridicule. Some adherents returned to their old churches. Some joined the Shakers, another New England–based doomsday sect that gained new members only through recruitment since they practiced celibacy. At least a dozen branches of Adventism grew out of Millerism, some almost overnight after the Great Disappointment, and many survive to this day. Ellen G. White, prophet and spiritual leader of the Seventh-day Adventist Church, which today claims 8.5 million members worldwide, later compared Miller to John the Baptist in her writing.

After October 22, 1844, Miller quit his active ministry, although he remained involved in Adventism. He still insisted the time was close at hand and he was cast out of the Baptist church in Low Hampton. Within three years he was blind. In May 1849, he was too sick to attend the Advent Conference in New York City. Instead, he sent a letter that said, "My belief is unshaken in the correctness of the conclusions I have arrived at. . . . We may not know the precise time, but I entreat of you all to be prepared for the approaching crisis."

He died seven months later, three days after Himes made a final visit. Miller, unable to speak for more than a few moments, proclaimed, "Elder Himes has come—I love Elder Himes." He told another deathbed visitor, "Tell them we are right. The coming of the Lord draweth nigh; but they must be patient, and wait for him."

Himes died in South Dakota in 1895, escaping "at last from the gibes and ridicule incurred by the failure of the prophecy" according to Sears. Fifteen years earlier, "he suddenly renounced the doctrine which he had been so instrumental in spreading and took orders as a clergyman of the Episcopal Church." Even though he became an Episcopalian in his later years, Himes carried at least one of the Millerites' 1844 beliefs to the grave—he asked his bishop to bury him in an elevated spot in Mount Pleasant Cemetery in Sioux Falls "because he wanted to be on the top of a hill when Gabriel blows his trumpet."

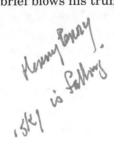

CHAPTER 7

Governor Henry J. Gardner
"Americanize America"

In 1840 about four thousand of Boston's ninety-three thousand residents were Irish. Ten years later, due to the Irish Potato Famine and the subsequent "clearing of the land" by British landlords, thirty-seven thousand of the city's residents—more than a quarter of all Bostonians—hailed from the Olde Sode.

And they just kept coming. By 1855 the number of Irish in Beantown had grown to more than fifty thousand. The arrival of the Irish would change Boston and America forever. Initially, those changes were only painful.

"The Irish are perhaps the only people in our history with the distinction of having a political party, the Know Nothings, formed against them," wrote then-Senator John F. Kennedy, the future president, in his 1958 book, *A Nation of Immigrants.*

The Massachusetts Know Nothings, led by Governor Henry J. Gardner, swept to power in 1854. Their platform was dotted with various reforms—ten-hour factory workdays, and support of temperance, abolition, and women's rights. Make no mistake, however, the party had one great aim—to repress the Irish in Massachusetts, and to, in Gardner's own inaugural words, "Americanize America." Guided by Gardner's vision that the Irish influx was the Commonwealth's main problem, the Know Nothing legislature passed laws between 1854–1857 that required the reading of the Protestant Bible in the public schools, banned the teaching of foreign languages, disbanded Irish militia units, established a special committee to inspect nunneries and convents, and forced the Irish off the state payroll. Several constitutional amendments also passed easily, including one forbidding Roman Catholics from holding public office in Massachusetts.

[handwritten margin note: might be akin to the Tea Party]

The Boston newspaper, the *Know Nothing and American Cru-sader,* gloried in the changes: "Old Massachusetts is thoroughly Americanized. . . . The Romish Harlot is on the defensive . . . death to all foreign influences."

Under a "pauper removal law" more than 1,300 destitute Irish men, women, and children in the state almshouses and in its asylums were rounded up and shipped back to Liverpool. One Boston newspaper trumpeted "these leeches upon our taxpayers" were across the ocean "where they belong."

Gardner and many of the Massachusetts Know Nothings claimed to be antislavery and enacted civil rights legislation while in power. That contradiction caught the attention of a future president.

"I do not perceive how anyone sensitive to the wrongs of the Negro can join in a league to degrade a class of white men," Abra-ham Lincoln wrote to a friend in 1855.

Part of the enmity was based in sheer numbers. In Boston the "Irish problem" resulted greatly because, unlike previous immigrants who arrived in Boston Harbor and moved west, the Irish—including JFK's great-grandfather, Patrick Kennedy, a farmer who had left County Wexford in 1849—stayed in the Hub.

"Two conditions were essential before a large immigrant group would stay in Boston," historian Oscar Handlin wrote. "First, the immigrants must be more interested in escaping from Europe than in what faced them in America. Secondly, they must have so little mobility that, once in Boston, they could not go elsewhere because poverty deprived them of the means, and despondence of the desire. For a long time this combination of factors did not apply to any migration that affected Boston. Most immigrants coming to America sought the fertile soil west of Boston, or the greater merchant and industrial opportunities found in other burgeoning American cities. Most had a little money to get to their desired destination. The potato famine in Ireland that began in 1845 changed all of that."

Of the eight million souls living in Ireland at the start of the famine, one million died of typhus or starvation—some with their mouths stained green because they tried to stay alive by eating grass—and about one million emigrated, most to America.

Boston's "famine Irish" settled in clannish ghettos along the waterfront and in the North End. Illiterate and unskilled—the British Parliament had earlier passed laws barring Irish peasants from attending school—they took whatever work they could find; many ended up on the public dole.

"Poor relief in Boston rose from $43,700 in 1845 to $137,000 in 1851, and over the same period the number of foreign-born paupers tripled, from four to twelve thousand," Jack Beatty wrote in *The Rascal King*. "Moralists worried over the proliferation of 'groggeries'—numbering 1,200 by 1849—where whiskey sold for twenty-eight cents a gallon. Drunkenness brought crime: between 1843 and 1848 'attempts to kill,' to use the language of the clerk of the Boston Police Court, went up by an unbelievable 1,700 percent; 'assaults on police officers,' by 400 percent; 'aggravated assaults' with weapons ranging from pistols to bricks, by 465 percent. Nativists were alarmed at the 200 percent surge in the Irish population between 1850 and 1855, compared with the feeble 15 percent blip in the non-Irish population."

The Yankees, who had run the city since the Puritans settled it in 1630, were troubled by the Irish's odd brogue, their out-of-date clothing, their fondness for whiskey and their poverty. They were especially repulsed by their Catholicism, and feared, as the Irish verged on becoming the majority, that the Pope in Rome would soon be setting Massachusetts's policy. The Irish Catholic's arrival was "about equivalent to a social revolution," according to Yankee historian Ephraim Peabody.

Immigration had helped the country grow, but unbridled it became a huge concern for white Protestant Americans during the mid-nineteenth century. Four hundred thousand immigrants arrived in the United States in 1854 alone. Almost three million arrived from 1844 to 1854—about one sixth of the 1845 population.

"Nativists complained that poor immigrants, particularly the Irish, overran the poorhouses and, along with the Germans,

THE PROPAGATION SOCIETY.___ MORE FREE THAN WELCOME.

A Know Nothing cartoon by Currier and Ives

contributed to intemperance and alcohol related problems, including crime, indigence, and violence," according to historian Ronald P. Formisano.

A backlash was inevitable, and nowhere was the backlash more severe than in Boston.

Boston today is one of the nation's most Irish and most Catholic cities, but that was not the case for more than two hundred years after the Puritans founded it. The early history of Massachusetts and the entire country is replete with a deep distrust of the Pope and with anti-Catholic sentiment. Even Declaration of Independence author Thomas Jefferson wrote, "History, I believe, furnishes no example of a priest-ridden people maintaining a free civil government," and "in every country and in every age, the priest has been hostile to liberty. He is always in alliance with the despot, abetting his abuses in return for protection to his own."

By the mid-nineteenth century, the arrival of many immigrants from Catholic countries turned the distrust into abject fear. In the 1830s Boston Presbyterian minister Lyman Beecher, the American Temperance Society cofounder and father of thirteen, including abolitionists Harriet Beecher Stowe and Henry Ward Beecher, constantly warned of the Catholic menace and the influence of the Pope.

"The Catholics have the perfect right to proselyte the nation to their faith if they are able to do it," he said. "But I have the right of preventing it if I am able."

Beecher also pointed out that working-class Protestants feared losing their jobs to the Irish (just as the Irish would later fear losing their jobs to blacks).

"Our lower people hate the Irish," Beecher said, "because they keep their wages lower, are good at a fight, and they despise them for their ignorance, poverty, and superstition."

Beecher's anti-Catholic and anti-Irish sermons, along with fraudulent allegations that nuns were holding schoolgirls captive, inspired a mob of forty-five Protestant Boston workmen to burn the Ursuline Convent school in Charlestown to the ground in

1834. The state legislature refused to award the Catholic Diocese money to rebuild, and juries found all those accused of arson not guilty. When mob leader John Buzzell was acquitted, hundreds in the audience applauded, and as Buzzell exited the courtroom, people rushed up and congratulated him. Anti-Catholics also rioted in Bangor, Maine, that year.

That fear was the same, from New England to Florida and west to the territories. Many white Protestants saw a growing threat to their America from the "Papists."

Catholic. Illiterate. Dirt poor. Even the Irish who trickled into Massachusetts to work on railroads before the famine were shunned. Massachusetts Secretary of Education Horace Mann, "the father of public education," attracted the ire of landowners in the late 1830s by advocating for laws requiring towns to provide schooling for the hundreds of Irish children living in squatters' camps. Property owners whose taxes supported the schools—which is still the case in Massachusetts—were opposed to those laws.

"Every wise, humane measure adopted for [the immigrants'] welfare, directly promotes our own security," Mann responded. "The children of this people will soon possess the rights of men, whether they possess the characters of men or not."

The Nativist and anti-Catholic sentiments only deepened in the late 1840s and 1850s as boatload after boatload of immigrants arrived in Boston and New York. Signs began appearing in Boston employers' windows, "Irish Need Not Apply." In 1849 the Order of the Star Spangled Banner, the forerunner of the Know Nothings' American Party, was formed in New York. That same year, a bizarre dispute between supporters of American thespian Edwin Forrest and his British rival William Macready over who was a better Shakespearian actor—and enflamed by anti-British feelings over an ongoing Oregon territory dispute—attracted a crowd of several thousand Nativists to Astor Place Opera House in New York City. Riots ensued. Police fired into the crowd and twenty-three Nativists died.

In 1851 in Providence, Rhode Island, a Nativist mob attacked a Sisters of Mercy convent and broke all the windows. They returned days later, intent on razing the building, according to Peter Condon in 1910's *Catholic Encyclopedia,* but dispersed after "finding it guarded by a number of Catholic Irishmen, with Bishop O'Reilly present and declaring that the sisters and their convent should be protected at whatever cost." In 1853 the visit to America of Archbishop Bedini, Apostolic Nuncio to the Court of Brazil, was marked by protests in Boston, Baltimore, Wheeling, St. Louis, and Cincinnati. A mob of six hundred men armed with weapons and carrying torches and ropes marched to the cathedral in Cincinnati, intending to set it on fire and hang the Nuncio. Police quelled the rioters but not until after shots had been fired and several people were wounded.

Meanwhile, a new political movement was starting in Massachusetts and elsewhere. Know Nothingism spread like wildfire, burned white hot for a few years, and then disappeared.

"Divided into lodges, linked by passwords and special handshakes, the secret society took its name from the answer its members gave to queries about its purpose: 'I know nothing about it,'" Beatty wrote. "Officially, the Know Nothings would be called the American Party, but in the months before it surfaced in the election of 1854, the secret society was identified by its members only by a code name, Sam. Membership in Sam was reserved for native-born Americans, Protestants 'born of Protestant parents, reared under Protestant influence, and not united in marriage with a Roman Catholic.' These were not strenuous criteria in Massachusetts; virtually every nonimmigrant resident could meet them. Consequently, the Know Nothings quickly became a mass, albeit still clandestine, movement."

In Massachusetts the leader of the Know Nothings was a dry goods merchant named Henry J. Gardner. He was born in the Dorchester section of Boston on June 14, 1818, the son of Dr. Henry and Clarissa (Holbrook) Gardner. Gardner attended private schools, graduating from Philip Exeter Academy in New

Hampshire. According to Harvard University president Edward Everett, Gardner then became "a wild youth at college: was suspended, went home to his father and was rebuked . . . ran away and went to sea as a common sailor; and returned reformed and industrious." He returned to school and graduated from Bowdoin College in Maine in 1838. He became a partner in a Boston dry goods company and eventually bought out his partner, renaming the business Henry J. Gardner & Company. He married Helen Cobb in 1843 and they had four sons and three daughters.

He first entered politics at the age of thirty-two, serving as a member of the Boston Common Council in 1850–1854, and as its president in 1852 and 1853. He served in the Massachusetts House of Representatives in 1851–1852, and on the Whig State Central Committee in 1853–1854. The Whig party was in decline, though, and Gardner secretly became a Know Nothing. When the American Party suddenly emerged for the 1854 elections, Gardner became a candidate.

"While known as a conservative [Whig] of the Daniel Webster school, Gardner broke with that faction by participating in an [antislavery] meeting earlier in 1854," wrote Tyler Anbinder in his 1992 book, *Nativism and Slavery: The Northern Know Nothings and the Politics of the 1850s*. "Know Nothing leaders in Massachusetts were primarily conservatives who could not stomach [Republican gubernatorial candidate Henry] Wilson's radicalism on the slavery issue. They therefore turned to Gardner—a moderate, experienced politician not well known outside Boston—to head the Know-Nothing ticket."

The Know Nothing leaders realized they needed the state's large antislavery bloc of voters to ensure Gardner's victory. They made a deal with Wilson, who had also secretly joined the Know Nothings, to ensure the support of his followers. Wilson agreed to decline the Republican nomination just days before the election to make sure his party would not be able to field a suitable replacement candidate, and in return the Know Nothings legislators would vote for him for US Senator. (Before the 17th Admendment passed in 1912, US senators were elected by state legislatures.) It worked. Wilson, who reidentified himself as a Republican in 1856, would spend eighteen prolific years in the Senate before serving as Ulysses S. Grant's second vice president, but he never completely lived down the double dealing of that 1854 election.

In his own campaign, Gardner painted himself as an abolitionist as well as a teetotaling xenophobe. The Kansas-Nebraska Act was being heavily debated throughout the nation that year. That act created the territories of Kansas and Nebraska, opening new lands for settlement and allowing settlers in those territories to determine through popular sovereignty whether they would allow slavery. Slavery proponents and opponents poured into Kansas and Nebraska and bloody strife ensued in both territories. In-party division on the question of the day—slavery—led to the downfall of the Whigs and eventually also led to the downfall of the Know Nothings.

"Opponents charged that it was not safe to vote for Gardner because neither he nor any other Know Nothing candidate had taken a public stand on the issues," Anbinder wrote. "Know Nothings replied that the Order in Massachusetts opposed the Kansas-Nebraska Act and supported temperance. . . . To bolster his anti-slavery image, Gardner pointed out that he had proposed that Whigs support an anti-Nebraska fusion ticket, but that the Whig State Committee had rejected his proposal. Gardner attributed his abandonment of the Whig party to this defeat, and he called himself the most strongly anti-slavery candidate in the field."

While the American Party was divided on the issue of slavery, it was not on the issue of Irish Catholic naturalization. Fueled by fear of Irish and German immigration, the Know Nothings' popularity spread like wildfire and in the general elections on November 13, 1854, their candidates swept to victory, especially in Massachusetts. Gardner, with 81,503 votes, hammered the Whig incumbent and the Democrat and Republican candidates, who garnered 47,504 votes between them.

The heretofore-unknown Know Nothings had previously tasted some success in the municipal elections held around Massachusetts in the spring. Know Nothing candidates won offices in Salem and Cambridge then; and in Boston, Know Nothing J. V. C. Smith won the largest vote ever cast for mayor.

Still, no one could have predicted what would happen just a few months later.

It rained heavily during the fall general election on November 13, but that did nothing to hinder the Nativist turnout across the Bay State. "It poured water and Know Nothings all day," according to one newspaper. The Know Nothings swept every state constitutional office and won all forty state Senate races and every US Congressional district. They won all but two of the 381 seats in the state House of Representatives. Gardner carried every city in the Commonwealth.

The country was stunned by the Know Nothings' victories. The Know Nothings enjoyed success elsewhere in 1854—electing mayors in Philadelphia, Washington, DC, and San Francisco, and the governor of California—but nowhere was their success as great as in Massachusetts.

"Who was so wild, or so enthusiastic, as to dream that a party unheard of at the last election, with a self-chosen cognomen as ridiculous as satire itself could invent, . . . and burrowing in secret like a mole in the dark, would suddenly spring up, snap asunder the strongest ties of party, enlist under its banner the most incongruous elements, absorb the elective strength of the state, and carry everything before it, . . . leaving only the smallest fragments of the three parties which were struggling for supremacy?" William Lloyd Garrison's *Liberator* asked. "Nothing like it can be found in the political history of the country. Even now, with the figures staring us in the face, it seems almost incredible."

In his inaugural speech as governor, Gardner vowed to "Americanize America." He said he would seek a constitutional amendment that would exclude naturalized citizens from public office. He also called for a strict literacy test and a twenty-one-year residency requirement before naturalized immigrants would be allowed to vote. Americans, Gardner said, must "nationalize before we naturalize."

The Know Nothings' own newspaper editorialized on the reasons for Gardner's call for a longer naturalization process.

"Foreigners are made . . . 'American citizens' altogether too rapidly," the *Know Nothing and American Crusader* reasoned. "Raw, verdant, outlandish fellows, fresh from the emigrant ship, with no more comprehension of the duties of a citizen; no more knowledge of our government; no more fitness to act the great character of a Republican than a Chinese automaton, are daily, by the thousands, metamorphosed into the stature and privileges of full American citizenship."

After the victories in 1854, the Know Nothings officially adopted the American Party name. Attacks on Catholics increased in frequency. That year, a priest, Father John Bapst, was tarred and feathered and ridden out of Ellsworth, Maine, on a rail. Also, in 1854, a traveling street preacher named James Orr incited a mob of one thousand to attack the Irish Catholics' church in nearby Bath, Maine. The rioters hoisted an American flag into the belfry, rang the bell, smashed the pews and set the church on fire. When the parishioners and their bishop attempted to lay a cornerstone for a new church a year later, the mob returned, and beat and chased the Catholics away.

Know Nothing mobs also attacked Catholic churches in New Jersey, Ohio, New York, Texas, and Connecticut, and in Lawrence and Chelsea, Massachusetts. In the Dorchester section of Boston, a keg of gunpowder was placed under the floor of a little Catholic church, Condon wrote, and then "it was fired at three o'clock in the morning and resulted in almost the total destruction of the building."

In one of his first acts in office, Gardner disbanded seven companies in the state militia composed primarily of immigrants. In Connecticut, William T. Minor—elected in 1855 along with seven other Know Nothing governors that year—disbanded the state's six Irish militia units.

"Sometimes the Know Nothings' zeal to promote 'Americanism' and fight Catholicism drove them to absurd lengths, especially in Massachusetts," Anbinder wrote. "In their fervor to Americanize the state's public institutions, the Bay State Know Nothings replaced the Latin inscription above the House Speaker's podium with an English translation. The legislators also barred the teaching of foreign languages in Massachusetts public schools. Their most outrageous act, however, involved the creation of a 'nunnery committee.'"

Nativists around the country had long suspected that Catholic priests were foisting themselves on young nuns in convents. Know Nothings in both Maryland and Massachusetts created committees to oversee the inspection of convents. A Whig newspaper soon accused Massachusetts's committee members of barging into convent rooms, intimidating and even propositioning nuns during their inspections. Nativists responded the inspections required surprise visits and private interviews with the nuns and novices. The ensuing investigation revealed that the committee's chairman, Joseph Hiss, had lodged a prostitute in the committee's hotel at the taxpayers' expense.

Gardner was reelected in 1855 and 1856. When they weren't busy persecuting Irish Catholics, the Massachusetts Know Nothing legislature pushed true reforms. It made vaccinations for schoolchildren compulsory, required youths working in factories to attend school a minimum of twelve weeks a year, passed several laws making wives more equal partners in their marriages, and issued the first racial desegregation law in the nation. The Massachusetts Irish feared the economic consequences of abolition; according to Handlin, they valued "the security that came from the existence in the country of at least one social class beneath them."

The American Party held its first and only national convention in 1856 in Philadelphia, where delegates supported former President Millard Fillmore as their presidential candidate. Gardner was considered for the vice presidency but chose to run for reelection instead. The Know Nothings were already losing their power, though, and their inability to agree on the subject of slavery soon spelled their end. During the convention, a group of antislavery delegates angrily left the floor. Henry Wilson, the US senator who was elected as a Know Nothing in 1854 after he dropped out of the Massachusetts governor's race, quit the party, saying he "had no sympathy with the narrow, bigoted, intolerant spirit that would make war on a race of men because they happen to be born in other lands . . . it is criminal fanaticism to oppress the Celt or the German." More pressing, though, he called the American Party, "broken and splintered to atoms by its failure on the question of abolition."

In the November election Fillmore received 21 percent of the popular vote and eight electoral votes, finishing third behind Democrat James Buchanan and Republican John Fremont.

Like Wilson, many antislavery Know Nothings joined the emerging Republican Party, while proslavery Know Nothings joined the Democrats. By 1858, the Know Nothing movement was no longer of any significance on the national stage. In his bid for a fourth term in 1857, Gardner finished a distant second to Republican Nathaniel Banks. After leaving office on January 6, 1858, Gardner returned to his dry goods business. He retired from the firm in 1876 and spent the remainder of his life as an agent of the Massachusetts Life Insurance Company. Gardner died at his home in Milton on July 21, 1892.

The Massachusetts Know Nothing movement burst and fizzled like a bottle rocket on the Fourth of July. It was, according to Ralph Waldo Emerson, an "abdication of reason . . . an immense joke." The Know Nothings' legacy, however, left a deep mark on the Commonwealth. The Irish never forgot how they had been treated at the hands of the Know Nothing abolitionists. They flocked to the Democratic Party. In the presidential election of 1860, Boston's Irish wards voted overwhelmingly for Stephen Douglas over Republican Abraham Lincoln. Massachusetts's Sons of Erin fought valiantly in the Civil War, but they fought to preserve the Union, not to end slavery.

When it became obvious in the late 1850s that the Know Nothings were finished as a force in the North, many rejoiced. The *New York Times,* however, urged caution.

"No sentiment, or conviction, which has the power to create such a party in so short a time, can perish or lose its vital force so suddenly," the *Times* sagely warned.

Within a decade, a new secret society that included hatred for Catholics and immigrants, as well as blacks, would don its sheets in the South and spread north.

CHAPTER 8

Jane Toppan
"Jolly Jane" killed them all

Jane Toppan was morbidly obese, abandoned to an orphanage by her drunk and abusive father, and unloved and humiliated by her foster mother.

Is that why the Boston nurse injected at least thirty-one people—and possibly many more–with morphine overdoses? Is that why she was sexually aroused while holding their dying bodies close to her corpulent self as they shuttered and rattled in death?

Was "Jolly Jane" a criminal—or just totally bonkers?

That was the question everyone around the nation was asking after Toppan was arrested for the murder of four members of the Davis family in a six-week span during the summer of 1901. Prestigious medical publications such as the *Boston Medical and Surgical Journal* weighed in before her 1902 trial.

"She is alleged to have stated, although the fact was not brought out in court, that she is a sexual pervert and got gratification from murder," Dr. George Shattuck, editor of the *Journal* wrote. "(However) the number of sexual perverts in the community is very large and that symptom is not sufficient to constitute a degenerate."

Shattuck went on to say he would not render an opinion on Toppan's responsibility until all the evidence was presented, but "we do feel sure that a hospital for the insane is not a secure enough place for a criminal of Jane Toppan's type, and urge that she be held in a prison or asylum for the criminally insane."

The trial lasted only eight hours on June 23, 1902, and the jury took only twenty minutes to find Toppan not guilty by reason of insanity. She had already confessed to thirty-one murders and expressed no remorse. She said she wished that she had been able to keep going. Toppan told the investigators she got "voluptuous delight" and "irresistible sexual impulse" from overdosing people and crawling into bed with them as they passed away.

Investigators believed she actually killed far more than the thirty-one about whom she could give them details. She almost always used a combination of morphine and atropine (to mask the effects of the morphine).

"That is my ambition, to have killed more people—more helpless people—than any man or woman who has ever lived," she told investigators. "Yes, I killed all of them. I fooled them all—I fooled the stupid doctors and the ignorant relatives. I have been fooling them all for years and years."

Female serial killers are rare compared to male serial killers, and a female serial killer who murders for sexual kicks is even rarer.

"There has been little to no research on female lust killers, in part because it's an unexpected phenomenon and in part because the cases are rare," Katherine Ramsland wrote in *The Forensic Examiner* in 2007. "However, similar to male lust murder, the female counterpart is often driven by a paraphilia, such as arousal upon viewing a corpse or when rubbing inappropriately against someone. Often, there's something deviant in their sexual development that consistently triggers arousal and thus feeds a compulsion."

"Jolly Jane" Toppan had plenty of deviancy in her development.

Born Honora "Nora" Kelley in Boston in 1857, she was the third daughter of Irish Famine immigrants Pete and Bridget Kelley. Pete Kelley was an alcoholic tailor and an abusive man. Bridget died of tuberculosis when Jane was a baby. Like almost all of the Irish who had flooded Boston in the decade after the 1845–1850 potato famine, the Kelleys lived in wretched poverty, compounded in their home by alcoholism and mental illness. Honora's oldest sister Nellie ended up in an insane asylum and Pete was eventually committed too. He was prone to violent outbursts and erratic behavior—his nickname in the neighborhood was "Kelley the Crack(pot)." After Bridget died, he was found one day in the tailor shop trying to sew his eyelids together. In 1863 he left six-year-old Nora and her eight-year-old sister Delia in the Boston Female Asylum, an institution for orphaned and needy girls. He never saw them again.

Two years later, Nora was placed as a live-in indentured servant to Mrs. Abner Toppan, a middle-aged widow from Lowell. (Delia remained in the orphanage for three more years before she was placed in a home in New York. Delia eventually became a prostitute and alcoholic and died in poverty.) Mrs. Toppan had a pretty daughter, Elizabeth, about Nora's age. Nora would become intensely jealous of Elizabeth even though, unlike Mrs. Toppan who humiliated and beat her, Elizabeth was always kind to Nora. Mrs. Toppan never formally adopted Nora but did change her name to Jane Toppan.

"Her position in the household was always equivocal," wrote Queens College professor Harold Schechter in *The Serial Killer Files*. "On the one hand, she was treated as a member of the family. On the other, she was never allowed to forget her lowly origins or her place as a menial. Within the community, her dark Irish looks branded her a permanent outsider. After a childhood of abuse, rejection, and abandonment, she grew up in a constant state of humiliation. It was the perfect recipe for the making of a psychopath."

Jane soon started gaining weight while living with the Toppans. (She eventually carried 209 pounds on her five-foot-three frame.) She also spread malicious rumors about people she envied, including Elizabeth, and set small fires. "Jane denied her Irish heritage by making derogatory anti-Irish and anti-Catholic statements in the Protestant circles in which she moved," according to Emily Allen, Alana Averill, and Emmeline Cook, researchers at Radford College's Department of Psychology.

Some of Jane's schoolmates despised her as a big fat liar, but to most, the chubby schoolgirl presented a vivacious appearance, thus the nickname "Jolly Jane."

"Like others of her ilk, however, she had a hidden self that was hopelessly diseased," Schechter wrote. "Beneath her amiable exterior existed a poisonous well of malevolence, a deep, implacable longing to do harm."

When Jane turned eighteen, she was released from indenture but remained in the Toppan household for ten more years, working as a servant for Mrs. Toppan and, after Mrs. Toppan passed away, for Elizabeth and her husband Oramel Brigham, a young deacon in a local church.

Jane had only one romance as a young woman and even received an engagement ring from a Lowell office clerk. But the young man broke it off after he fell for his landlord's daughter, and Jane tried to commit suicide.

In 1887 Jane enrolled in the nursing program at Cambridge Hospital. She impressed the doctors with her abilities and pleasing personality. She also started her "scientific experiments," using different levels of morphine and atropine to alter patients' recovery time. If she liked patients, she would falsify their charts and give them drug doses to make them ill so they would have to stay in her care.

"It is speculated that Jane killed more than a dozen patients while working at Cambridge," according to the Radford College researchers. "One patient, Mrs. Amelia Phinney, lived to later tell the tale of Jane's maliciousness. After surgery, Jane administered some bitter tasting medicine to Amelia to help with her pain. As she was slipping into unconsciousness, she realized that Jane had gotten into bed with her and began kissing her all over her face. Luckily for Mrs. Phinney, Jane was startled by someone and hastily left the room. As Amelia gained consciousness the next day, she thought the incident had all been a dream and she checked out of the hospital, keeping her fears silent until she found out that Jane had been arrested in 1901."

Despite the patients' deaths and suspicions that Jane was also stealing, Cambridge Hospital doctors gave her glowing recommendations to receive further training at Massachusetts General Hospital in 1888. Her fellow nurses there disliked her and suspected that she was cavalier in assigning dosages of opiates. She left the ward without permission one night and was fired without receiving her nursing license, even though she had passed the final and her diploma was signed. She worked for a while as a private nurse and then returned to Cambridge Hospital in 1890. She was fired again in 1891 for administering opiates recklessly. She became a private nurse again.

In 1895 Jane poisoned her landlord Israel Dunham and then moved in with Dunham's wife, Lovey. In 1897 Jane poisoned Lovey Dunham.

In August 1899 Jane went on vacation on Cape Cod with her foster sister, Elizabeth Toppan Brigham. Jane slowly poisoned her and later told investigators that Elizabeth, who had always been kind to her, was the first victim that she hated. She told Elizabeth's husband Oramel Brigham that it was his wife's last wish for Jane to have her gold watch and chain. Oramel gave it to her and Jane pawned it.

In February 1900 Jane poisoned her friend, Myra Conners, with strychnine in order to take over her position as dining matron at the Theological School in Cambridge. She was later fired for stealing.

Toppan continued to pick off victims over the next year and a half, but in the summer of 1901 she hit a grand slam with the Davis family. The patriarch, Alden Davis, was an old friend and he rented Toppan a cottage in Cataumet, a village in Bourne on the Cape. Toppan fell behind in the rent and Davis's wife Mary took a train to Cambridge to collect. Jane gave Mary some doctored mineral water, and when Mary became sick, some morphine. For days she toyed with Mary, plunging her into comas and then reviving her.

"[Mary Davis] came back a week later in a pine box," wrote Evan J. Albright in *Cape Cod Confidential.* "As she was old and known to be in poor health, it was thought she had been overcome by the unusual heat wave that had engulfed New England. One of those who had been by Mary Davis's side at her death was daughter Genevieve. Genevieve asked Jane Toppan to accompany her and her dead mother back to Cape Cod for the funeral."

Big mistake.

Jane set several fires in the Davis's cottage but they were all quickly extinguished. She poisoned Genevieve next. No one suspected foul play because Genevieve had been greatly depressed by her mother's death and most thought she had committed suicide.

Toppan knocked off Alden Davis a few days later. Again, people didn't suspect foul play because, after all, he too was old and his health poor, and they figured the death of his wife and daughter was just too much.

A week later, the other daughter, Maryanne "Minnie" Gibbs, became sick and died. While Minnie was dying, her husband was at sea. When he returned, Captain Irving Gibbs could not believe that his heretofore healthy wife had died of natural causes or suicide. He contacted Dr. Edward S. Wood, an expert toxicologist and professor at Harvard Medical School, who started to investigate.

Toppan's serial killing career would soon be over. She had moved back to Lowell, where she was living with Brigham and his elderly sister, whom she was nursing. She was hoping to marry her former brother-in-law, but he threw her out after—you guessed it—his sister died. He also contacted the Middlesex County District Attorney. The Middlesex DA asked his counterpart on the Cape to exhume the two Davis daughters' bodies. Morphine poisoning was ruled the cause of both deaths.

Jane was arrested in Amherst, New Hampshire, and charged with the murder of Maryanne Gibbs. Her case created a huge stir around the country—causing many to question whether she was crazy or a criminal—since her confession to thirty more murders had already been made public. The trial itself lasted just eight hours. The jury took twenty minutes to deliberate before finding her not guilty by reason of insanity on June 23, 1902. She was committed to the Taunton Lunatic Hospital.

"In Toppan's case, there is reason to believe that she was spared the death penalty not because she was truly insane, but because a jury of Victorian gentlemen couldn't bring themselves to sentence a 'respectable' woman to the gallows," according to serial killer expert Schechter.

SKETCHES AT TRIAL OF JANE TOPPAN FOR MURDER AT BARNSTABLE.

Jane Toppan at her trial in a Boston newspaper sketch in 1902

Toppan had calmly confessed the thirty-one murders to her defense attorney and investigators while being held for trial, providing details about her sexual excitement in holding dying bodies. She acknowledged there might have been others that she could not remember well. The *Philadelphia Medical Journal* cautioned before the trial that Toppan's claims of dozens of murders was not to be believed and was probably a ploy to gain acquittal by reason of insanity. "She is a shrewd lunatic," the editor of the *Journal* wrote.

Her lawyer published Toppan's confession in William Randolph Hearst's *New York Journal* after the trial and acknowledged that Toppan had told him she hoped she would be found insane because she might be released some day.

Ever calm, even Toppan wondered why she felt no remorse.

"I feel absolutely the same as I always have," she said shortly after her imprisonment. "I might say I feel hilarious, but perhaps that expresses it too strongly. I do not know the feeling of fear and I do not know the feeling of remorse, although I understand perfectly what these words mean. But I cannot sense them at all. I do not seem to be able to realize the awfulness of the things I have done, though I realize very well what those awful things are. I try to picture it by saying to myself, 'I have poisoned Mary, my dear friend; I have poisoned Mrs. Gibbs, I have poisoned Mr. Davis,' but I seem incapable to realize the awfulness of it. Why don't I feel sorry and grieve over it? I don't know. I seem to have a sort of paralysis of thought and reason."

Insanity was prevalent in Toppan's family and Schechter points to her unloved childhood as the catalyst for her becoming a serial killer.

"Obviously there are millions of adopted children who grow up to be perfectly happy and well-adjusted adults," he wrote. "Still a surprising high percentage of serial killers have been raised in adoptive or foster homes. . . . Jane Toppan's father was an illiterate abusive drunk who stuck both his daughters in an orphanage after the death of his wife and never saw them again. . . . The belief (usually fully justified) that they have been rejected by their birth parents contributes to the sense of worthlessness and shame that typifies budding psychopaths. . . . The adoptive or foster homes that some children find themselves in can have a deeply pernicious effect on their developing personalities. . . . Though Jane Toppan was given the name of her foster family, she was never formally adopted and was made to feel like a permanent outsider in the only home she ever knew."

In 1904 the *New York Times* sent a reporter to the Taunton asylum to do a follow-up on Toppan. He found Toppan wasting away, the formerly rotund serial killer now gaunt and being force-fed because she was convinced the staff was trying to poison her meals and tea.

"Jane Toppan, the poisoner of 31 persons, after two and a half years confinement in the insane hospital here, is approaching—has reached—the secondary stage of her ailment, moral insanity, and is believed to be near her end," the *Times* reported on October 23, 1904. "Her mental delusions are frequent, almost constant, and were anyone outside to see her, there would be no doubt of the appropriateness of her incarceration. She has abandoned the careless, cheerful frame of mind in which she has heretofore been, and is now fretful, peevish, even ugly, fault finding, fearful of eating because of suspected poison, complaining of her treatment, morose—everything but remorseful. The intellectual insanity, following the moral insanity with which it is now believed Jane Toppan has been afflicted with from birth, will in all probability result in her death, possibly within 12 months. She has dwindled to almost a skeleton."

The reporter's prediction of Toppan's impending demise was wrong. Jolly Jane started eating again and stayed confined in the Taunton asylum for thirty-four more years. She died there on August 17, 1938, never expressing any remorse but instead glorying in her crimes.

"According to legend, she would occasionally beckon to one of the nurses," Schechter wrote, "and, with a conspiratorial smile, say: 'Get the morphine, dearie, and we'll go out into the ward. You and I will have a lot of fun seeing them die.'"

CHAPTER 9

Judge Webster Thayer
Accused of "Judicial Homicide"

In 1908 two young men—one from the south of Italy and one from the north—arrived in America.

Although their names would soon become entwined in history, Bartolomeo Vanzetti and Nicola Sacco did not know each other then. They were, as Vanzetti later wrote, "nameless, in the crowd of nameless ones." Between 1880 and 1920, at least four million Italian immigrants arrived in the United States, the majority from 1900 to 1914. The Italians—with their dark skin, poverty, strange language, and their fondness for garlic, Chianti, and radical politics—quickly became a despised and feared minority in Boston, Massachusetts, and around the nation.

Boston's Brahmins, already put off by the hundreds of thousands of Catholics from Ireland who had arrived in Massachusetts in the second half of the nineteenth century, were particularly fearful of these loud and passionate—and also Catholic—Italians. In 1895 Massachusetts Senator Henry Cabot Lodge began lobbying Congress to ban "inferior stocks" from America's shores. A year earlier, the Bay State's bluebloods and their Protestant wannabes had formed the Immigration Restriction League.

One of those blueblood wannabes was Judge Webster Thayer. His name would also be entwined with Sacco and Vanzetti's, and today, it remains synonymous with judicial bias.

"History has cast the white-haired judge as the great villain," reporter John Yemma wrote in the *Boston Globe* in 1999. "Even now, no assumptions are safe in the Sacco and Vanzetti case, not evidence, not testimony, not judicial impartiality. Especially not judicial impartiality. Copies of Sacco's and Vanzetti's death certificates . . . contain the most chilling words of all the millions that have been said in the case since 1920. Cause of death: 'Electric shock. Judicial homicide.' To millions of people around the world—especially to liberals, labor activists, and Italian-Americans in the 1920s and 1930s—judicial homicide sums up what Judge Webster Thayer of Dedham committed when he ordered the two men strapped into the electric chair in Charlestown State Prison."

Most of the destitute Italian immigrants who had arrived in Boston or New York at the turn of the century stayed in or around East Coast cities. Boston's North End, just decades earlier an enclave for Irish immigrants, soon became almost exclusively Italian. In 1880 the city had only 1,200 Italian-born residents. By 1920, more than 44,000 Italians were packed into the North End alone, which was less than a square mile.

"To 'Cold Roast Boston,' the Italians, aka 'Guineas,' 'Wops' and 'Dagos,' seemed strangely passionate people," Bruce Watson wrote in his book *Sacco & Vanzetti: The Men, the Murders and the Judgment of Mankind.* "Worse than their drink or diet, was the Italian propensity for crime. . . . In big cities, granite quarries, mining camps, wherever Italians toiled, stories circulated about a criminal society known as the 'Black Hand.' . . . The stereotype was not without roots. Hundreds of unsolved murders, with most victims being Italian immigrants, marred police blotters in cities along the eastern seaboard. Most Italians worked too hard to have time for criminal activity, yet the Mafia stereotype penetrated American society."

The Italian immigrants who arrived in "LaMerica," mostly from rural areas in southern Italy, were desperately poor. Most were illiterate and few had marketable skills. They were forced to take the poorest paying and most backbreaking jobs available. They were often exploited upon their arrival by the *"patroni,"* established Italian immigrants who spoke English and acted as intermediaries between the new arrivals and prospective employers, always for a price. From 1895 to 1908, thousands of Italian men just off the boat in Boston were taken in wagons by the *patroni* forty miles west to Clinton, Massachusetts, where they built the granite Wachusett Reservoir Dam, still the world's largest hand-dug dam.

"The tale is told that they came expecting that the streets were paved with gold, but found not only that they were not paved with gold but they were not paved at all and that they were expected to pave them," according to the Dante Alighieri Society of Massachusetts. The Italian immigrants ended up in coal mines in Pennsylvania and West Virginia, in sweatshop factories in Boston and New York City. Most of the 362 who died in the deadliest coal mine disaster in United States history, the 1907 Monongah mine explosion in West Virginia, were Italian immigrants. Many of the 146 young women who died in the 1911 Triangle Shirtwaist fire in New York City were also Italian.

The destitute Italians, who came to America seeking freedom and fairness, as well as streets of gold, had been victims of corrupt and ineffective government in their homeland for centuries. Many were already radicalized in their worldview. Many, like Sacco, a gifted shoe worker, and Vanzetti, a fish peddler, quickly came to see American society as also unfair. They both became subscribers to *Cronaca Souvesuvia,* an Italian-American anarchist newspaper. They met in 1917 after joining Gruppo Autonomo, an East Boston–based group of Galeanisiti, the followers of radical anarchist Luigi Galeani. On Galeani's orders, Sacco left his wife and son in Stoughton and Vanzetti his home in Plymouth to flee to Mexico to avoid the draft for World War I.

Webster Thayer's life traveled a different path. He was born in 1857 in Worcester, "a Thayer but not one of the 'right' Thayers," according to the writer Upton Sinclair. His family was definitely middle class—his father was a meat wholesaler—but "Web" Thayer longed all his life to be accepted by the bluebloods. He graduated from Worcester Academy, then Dartmouth, where, despite his wiry frame, he captained the football and baseball teams. He did not attend law school, but read law under the guidance of an attorney and he was admitted to the Massachusetts bar in 1882. He practiced in Worcester, mostly civil cases, and was active in politics.

He was elected as a Worcester alderman. The father of two ran for mayor as a Democrat in 1894, lost, and then became a Republican. Massachusetts Governor Samuel W. McCall, a Dartmouth classmate, appointed Thayer to the bench in 1917.

"Making his presence strongly felt in any courtroom, the judge rephrased attorneys' questions, endlessly cited legal precedent, and punctuated his remarks with nineteenth century locutions such as 'Mark you' and 'What say?'" Watson wrote. Despite his Ivy League education, his membership in the finest country clubs, and his desire to swim with the bluebloods, Thayer never lost his Worcester accent and the anarchists he hated were always "anurchists." Thayer seldom tried to conceal his disdain for the "anurchists," draft-dodgers, Reds, union members, and Bolshevists, and even on the bench he let it spill out.

In late April 1919 a plot by anarchists to mail bombs to the homes of judges who had convicted Wobblies (International Workers of the World union members), politicians, and tycoons, was foiled at the last minute, with the only casualty being a maid in Georgia, whose hands were blown off. On June 2, 1919, a former editor of *Cronaca Souvesuvia* blew himself up trying to place a bomb on the doorstep of Attorney General A. Mitchell Palmer in Washington, DC. Encouraged by Congress, Palmer immediately began to round up and deport Italian radicals across the nation, and a "Red Scare" similar to one engineered by Wisconsin Senator Joe McCarthy thirty years later soon gripped the nation. Without warning and without warrants, Palmer's men raided union offices and the headquarters of communist, socialist, and anarchist organizations. In December, Palmer's agents seized 249 resident aliens, including the radical writer Emma Goldman, and placed them on board the *Buford,* bound for the Soviet Union.

Thayer was not a target of a bomb, but his hatred of "anurchists" was heightened. "Oh how unfortunate that any such a doctrine, so destructive in its character and so revolutionary in all its tendencies, should ever have reached the sacred shores of these United States," he wrote. In April 1920, Thayer presided over a case in which the jury found Segris Zakoff not guilty of advocating anarchy. Thayer promptly lambasted the jurors. "How did you arrive at such a verdict?" he scolded. "Did you consider the information that the defendant gave to the police officers . . . that he was a Bolshevist and that there should be a revolution in this country?"

That same month, at 3 p.m. on April 15, paymaster Frederick Parmenter and his guard Alessandro Berardelli carried the Slater-Morrill Shoe Company payroll of $15,776 down the main street of South Braintree. Two men standing by a fence suddenly pulled out guns and fired on them. The gunmen snatched up the cash boxes dropped by the mortally wounded pair and jumped into a waiting Buick. The bandit gang, comprised of four or five men, sped away, throwing tacks into the road to flatten the tires of pursuers. Dozens of workers in the Slater-Morrill factory watched the drama through grimy windows; others observed the fast-moving scene from the street. They would later offer conflicting testimony on what they saw.

The getaway car was found fifteen miles away in a garage in Bridgewater. Police left it there as a trap. Three weeks later, Sacco and Vanzetti, along with Mike Boda and Richard Orciani, went to claim the car. Sacco and Vanzetti were arrested while Boda and Orciani escaped. Police were actually hoping to snare Boda, aka Mario Buda, a violent anarchist and career criminal they suspected in the Braintree holdup. Although originally not suspected, both Sacco and Vanzetti were carrying guns at the time of their arrest and when questioned by the authorities they lied to cover their anarchist activities. As a result, they were held and eventually indicted for the South Braintree crimes. Vanzetti was also charged with an earlier botched payroll holdup on Christmas Eve, 1919, at a shoe factory in Bridgewater. (Sacco's employer confirmed he had been working that day.)

Vanzetti was indicted on June 11, his thirty-second birthday, for the Bridgewater holdup. Thayer, still seething about the jury verdict in the Zakoff trial, was assigned to Vanzetti's trial and he made his hatred for the draft-dodging Vanzetti clear from the start. Despite a strong alibi supported by many witnesses that Vanzetti had been delivering eels, an Italian delicacy and Christmas tradition, to his customers in Plymouth on December 24, he was found guilty. Most of Vanzetti's witnesses were Italians who spoke English poorly and failed to convince the all-American jury influenced by Thayer's harsh guidance. Vanzetti, on the advice of his attorney who feared he'd reveal his radical activities, did not take the stand in his own defense. Despite it being his first arrest and a dubious case at best—one prosecution witness testified that the gunman "ran like a foreigner"—Thayer sentenced Vanzetti to the maximum ten to fifteen years.

Thayer then asked to be assigned to the South Braintree trial to be held in the Dedham courthouse. Sacco and Vanzetti were indicted on September 11. In retaliation, Buda, still at large, blew up a bomb in Manhattan on September 16, killing thirty-eight and injuring more than two hundred. A new legal counsel was brought in to represent Sacco and Vanzetti. Fred H. Moore was a well-known socialist lawyer from out west who had collaborated in many labor and IWW trials. Thayer hated him from the start. Referring to Moore's frequent objections during the trial, he told reporters, "No long-haired anarchist from California can run this court." By trial's end, one of those reporters would write a letter to the state's attorney general decrying Thayer's prejudice.

"Whenever Moore addressed the judge, (co-counsel) Thomas McAnarney recalled, 'it was quite similar to waving a red flag in the face of a wolf . . . Mr. Moore would make an objection or make some remark and it would be perfectly clear that it got under Judge Thayer's skin,'" Watson wrote.

Moore decided to acknowledge Sacco and Vanzetti's anarchist leanings and tried to establish that their arrest and prosecution stemmed from their radical activities, despite the prosecution's insistence that only nonpolitical evidence had implicated the two men in the robbery and murder.

Moore organized public meetings, enlisted the support of labor unions, rallied international organizations, initiated investigations, and distributed thousands of pro-defense pamphlets throughout the United States and world. His strategy transformed a little-known case—violent robberies were common in America immediately after World War I and at the beginning of Prohibition— into an international cause célèbre.

Whenever Moore played his political card during the six-and-a-half-week trial, Thayer trumped him, and to many neutral observers, he seemed to be leading the jury—all white Protestant or Irish men—toward a conviction. William Thompson, who later took over Sacco and Vanzetti's appeal, noted that Thayer would raise his eyebrows and address Moore in sarcastic tones. "Your goose is cooked," he told McAnarney. Although jurors would later say they found Thayer to be scrupulously fair, future US Supreme Court justice Felix Frankfurter called Thayer's charge to the jury jingoistic and highly prejudicial. Thayer's instruction to jurors included many references to the duty and heroism of soldiers—the jurors were well aware that the defendants sitting in a steel cage had been draft dodgers—and he urged them to remember their "loyalty" and their "true American citizenship."

After often-conflicting testimony by 167 witnesses filled 2,266 pages of transcript, the jury found Sacco and Vanzetti guilty of robbery and murder on July 14, 1921. The guilty verdict marked the beginning of a six-year international struggle to save the two men. During that time, Thayer consistently denied every appeal by the defense for a new trial. The motions he denied included evidence of perjury by prosecution witnesses, of biased statements made by the jury foreman, of illegal activities and evidence tampering by police and federal authorities, a confession to the Braintree crimes by convicted bank robber Celestino Madeiros, and evidence that the notorious Morelli Gang was involved in the robbery. All motions were ruled on and rejected by Thayer. He even ruled on a motion accusing him of judicial prejudice.

Thayer's conduct during the trials and the appeals became a huge part of the controversy. In 1924 Thayer asked a lawyer acquaintance at a Dartmouth football game, "Did you see what

SACCO FLAYS CAPITALISTS IN FIERY SPEECH IN COURT

Holds Courtroom Spellbound by Address---Went to Mexico to Escape War Service, He States--- Proud of Having Been a Slacker

An editorial cartoon published during the 1921 trial

I did to those anarchist bastards the other day? I guess that will hold them for a while."

Frankfurter, then a law professor at Harvard University, published a scathing critique of the criminal case in the *Atlantic Monthly* in 1927.

"Every reasonable probability points away from Sacco and Vanzetti," Frankfurter wrote. "Every reasonable probability points toward the Morelli gang."

Sacco and Vanzetti became disenchanted with Moore's effort to save them. They thought he spent their defense fund, built with quarters and dollars donated from people around the world, too freely. He had also made some curious trial decisions, agreeing, for example, to strike from the record all testimony that his clients "bore the reputation of being peaceful and law-abiding citizens." In 1924 they replaced him with Thompson, a Boston lawyer who assumed control of the legal defense for the last three years of the case. Thompson, a Brahmin, had no sympathy for the anarchist ideas of the two men, "half-educated dreamers and fanatics," but he came to admire them deeply as individuals. Also a Worcester native, Thompson had known Thayer all his life and found him "full of prejudice [and] carried away with this fear of Reds." Thompson argued for a new trial before the Supreme Judicial Court of Massachusetts twice, in 1926 and in 1927, but the high court declined to reopen the case.

Protests increased around the world. Albert Einstein, George Bernard Shaw, H. G. Wells, Edna St. Vincent Millay, Upton Sinclair, and John Dos Passos were among the celebrities that rallied to the cause. The writer and actor Robert Benchley, a Worcester native, created a huge stir when he filed an affidavit in early 1927 that was soon reprinted in the *Boston Evening Transcript*.

"My name is Robert Benchley. I reside in the city of New York. I was brought up in the city of Worcester and am acquainted with many people there among others with Mr. Loring Coes . . . In the year 1921 I was sitting in an automobile outside the Worcester Golf Club waiting for Mr. Coes to come out. When Mr. Coes came

out . . . he told us what Judge Thayer had just said in his presence. . . . Mr. Coes told us what Judge Thayer had just been telling, what he, Judge Thayer, intended to do to Sacco and Vanzetti,
whom Judge Thayer referred to as 'those bastards down there.' Mr.
Coes said that Judge Thayer had referred to Sacco and Vanzetti as
Bolsheviki who were 'trying to intimidate him' and said that 'he
would get them good and proper.'" Coes swiftly denied everything
that Benchley said.

Thayer, meanwhile, became a hero to conservatives and self-
styled patriots who wanted to defend the honor of American justice and the "American way of life." The Worcester Bar Association
gave Thayer a plaque thanking the sixty-nine-year-old jurist for
his resolute behavior in the case, even after the *Boston Herald*
won a Pulitzer Prize for an editorial blasting Thayer for being "the
advocate rather than the arbitrator."

On April 9, 1927, after all appeals had failed, Thayer sentenced Sacco and Vanzetti to death. Workers in the world's great
cities—including Paris, London, Mexico City, and Buenos Aires—
protested the unfairness of their trial. Massachusetts Governor
Alvan T. Fuller even went to the prisons to interview the two men
as he considered executive clemency. He appointed an advisory
committee headed by A. Lawrence Lowell, president of Harvard
University. The committee concluded that the trial and judicial
process had been just "on the whole" and that clemency was
not warranted. The committee did have some harsh criticism
for Thayer. "He ought not to have talked about the case off the
bench, and doing so was a grave breach of judicial decorum," the
report said. They determined, however, that anything he said had
no impact on the trial. The trial transcript, the committee said,
showed Thayer "tried to be scrupulously fair" and reported that
the jurors were almost unanimous in praising Thayer's conduct
of the trial.

The execution was set for midnight on August 22, 1927. At 3
a.m. on August 16, a bomb exploded at the home of one of the Dedham jurors, causing extensive damage but no injuries. On Sunday,

August 21, more than twenty thousand protesters assembled on Boston Common.

On the night of the executions, state police set up machine guns atop the walls of the prison, now the site of Bunker Hill Community College, to keep watch over the blocked-off streets, and gunboats patrolled Boston Harbor. Sacco and Vanzetti were executed at the appointed hour, moments after Madeiros, who was executed for another murder but had been kept alive in case his testimony would be needed in a Sacco-Vanzetti appeal. Sacco was next. His last words were "Viva l'anarchia!" and "Farewell, mother." Vanzetti shook hands with guards and thanked them for their kindness, read a statement proclaiming his innocence, and added, "I wish to forgive some people for what they are now doing to me." People from as far away as Beacon Hill watched the distant lights on the Charlestown prison flicker then surge as each man was electrocuted.

Violent demonstrations swept through Geneva, London, Paris, Amsterdam, Johannesburg, and Tokyo the next day. Wild-cat strikes closed South American factories. At Langone Funeral Home in the North End, Sacco and Vanzetti were laid out in open caskets under a wreath that said ASPETTANDO L'ORA DELLA VENDETTA (awaiting the hour of vengeance). More than one hundred thousand viewers filed by over the next two days. A fifteen-minute battle between mourners and police marred a two-hour funeral procession through the city to Forest Hills Cemetery on August 28.

Sporadic anarchist bombings continued in retaliation around the world, including at the home of another of the Dedham jurors and on the front porch of the executioner, state electrician Robert Elliott. No one was injured in either of those incidents. Thayer, described by one magazine as "the peacetime soldier fighting for his country," fearlessly reveled in his celebrity and often spoke at public gatherings, acknowledging standing ovations with a tip of his fedora. On September 27, 1932, Thayer's home in Worcester was destroyed and his wife and housekeeper slightly injured by a bomb blast. "I hate to think that because a man does his duty before mankind and God that the penalty is this," he told the *Boston Evening Globe*. Thayer then moved into his club in Boston, where he was guarded twenty-four hours a day until suffering a fatal stroke seven months later.

Thayer believed that Sacco and Vanzetti were guilty until his dying day. Thompson remained certain they were not.

"It is pointless to debate their guilt or innocence," Peter W. Agnes Jr., presiding judge of Charlestown District Court and an expert on the case, told the *Boston Globe* in 1999. "Whether they were or were not responsible for murder, they did not receive a fair trial, in part because of popular hysteria, a biased judge, and a flawed legal system."

On the fiftieth anniversary of the executions, Governor Michael S. Dukakis issued a proclamation declaring "any stigma and disgrace should be forever removed from the names of Nicola Sacco and Bartolomeo Vanzetti, from the names of their families and descendants, and so . . . [I] call upon all the people of Massachusetts to pause in their daily endeavors to reflect upon these tragic events, and draw from their historic lessons the resolve to prevent the forces of intolerance, fear, and hatred from ever again uniting to overcome the rationality, wisdom, and fairness to which our legal system aspires."

CHAPTER 10

J. Franklin Chase
"The Guardian of the Purity of the Puritans"

The term "Banned in Boston" did not enter the national lexicon until the 1920s, but censorship had flourished in Beantown from the start.

It has often been said that the Puritans in Boston and their self-righteous doppelgangers, the Pilgrims in Plymouth, "would lie awake worrying that someone somewhere was having a good time." Both the Puritans and Pilgrims expelled the cavalier Thomas Morton, who in 1624 had established the freewheeling Merrymount plantation in what is now the Wollaston section of Quincy. The Pilgrims first shipped him back to England in 1628 after Plymouth Governor William Bradford sent Captain Myles Standish to arrest Morton for, among other things, composing "sundry rhymes and verses, some tending to lasciviousness," and "quaffing & drinking both wine & strong waters in great exsess, and, . . . drinking and dancing aboute [a maypole] many days togeather, inviting the Indean women, for their consorts, dancing and frisking together."

Morton was back in Massachusetts within two years. He was arrested again in 1630, this time by Governor John Winthrop of the rapidly growing Massachusetts Bay Puritan colony in Boston. Winthrop ordered Merrymount burned to the ground. Puritan leader John Endicott also marched from Salem to cut down the maypole that Morton, his followers, and their Native American girlfriends had partied around.

Morton stayed in England for twelve years and wrote a book, *New English Canaan,* about his experiences in Massachusetts, referring to the vertically challenged Standish as "Captain Shrimp" throughout and happily aiming to get the Pilgrim's and

Puritan's noses "out of joynt." He also tried to get the Massachusetts Bay charter revoked while in England. When Morton got
back to Massachusetts, Winthrop noted in his journal that "our
professed old adversary, who had set forth a book against us and
had written reproachful and menacing letters to some of us" had
returned. Winthrop gave Morton the boot again—this time he
went to the coast of Maine, outside the Massachusetts jurisdiction,
and lived there until he died four years later.

Fast forward three centuries. It's 1925 and the Boston Brahmins, many of them directly descended from the Puritans, are lying
awake worrying that some school boy in Dorchester or Fitchburg
is masturbating while he reads Sherwood Anderson's *Many Marriages* or John Dos Passos's *Streets of Night*. They are members of
the Watch and Ward Society, some of them are Protestant clergy,
and they are joined in a curious alliance by the Irish Catholics, the
new majority in Boston, whom they have long despised but with
whom they share an abiding fear of S-E-X.

Their main man is a pit bull guarding the public decency. His
name is J. Franklin Chase and he has enormous influence over
government officials, bookstore owners, and the police. Unlike
the founders and most current members of the Watch and Ward,
Chase is not a Brahmin. He grew up in a tough neighborhood in
Chelsea, bragged that he "licked every red-headed (Irish) man"
there—and even as an adult always leads with his fists. His blue-
blooded employers—the Cabots and Lodges and Longfellows—
tolerate him, though, because of his aggressive approach to make
Boston "the cleanest city" in America.

Chase gladly takes on all evils—prostitutes, gamblers, burlesque
performers and theater owners, booksellers and magazine publishers—but mostly leaves alcohol to numerous temperance organizations and, in the 1920s, to government agents enforcing Prohibition.
He is so cocky that he even consents to an interview with A. L. S.
Wood from *American Mercury* magazine, which is published by noted
libertarian H. L. Mencken. Wood's subsequent article in the September 1925 edition, "Keeping the Puritans Pure," drips with sarcasm.

In the opening paragraph, Wood describes Chase, then fifty-three, as tall, thickset and "obviously healthy." His thin white hair is tousled, he is bespectacled and "his grizzled moustache of walrus design masks a virtuous mouth." He is smoking a cigar ironically called "Between the Acts" in his Park Square office. Chase is dictating a letter about miscreants who have been caught selling *The Memories of a Young Girl* and "inflammatory pictures" to high school boys in Fitchburg and Worcester.

"So there, smoking a 'Between the Acts,' with his feet on his desk, sat the guardian of the purity of the Puritans," Wood wrote. "The major premise of the Rev. Mr. Chase's philosophy is that all excitation of the sexual impulse is evil. His minor premise is that 'bad' books excite it."

Chase was born in Boston, on March 7, 1872. His parents were Jason and Emma Chase. He was baptized Jason Franklin but he later abbreviated his first name to an initial. He graduated from Wesleyan University in Middletown, Connecticut, in 1899, and then from Boston University's School of Theology in 1901. He was ordained a Methodist minister and served as pastor in churches in Essex, West Roxbury, and Allston. When he left his West Roxbury ministry, his congregation gave the Reverend Chase and his wife a trip to Italy. While in Florence, after "repulsing an insistent peddler of degenerate photographs, I acquired the conviction that took me out of a pulpit and put me in a forum." In 1907 while pastor in Allston, he was offered the job as secretary of the New England Watch and Ward Society. "It struck me that the Watch and Ward Society offered a great field for a man who was rough and ready," he later said. His job was to root out bad moral influences and he performed it with relish.

"Wine, women and song, with all their collateral evils, are the province of the Secretary of the New England Watch and Ward Society," Wood wrote. Chase also went after gamblers, opium dens, and cocaine and morphine dealers.

The New England Society had been born in 1878, when four hundred to five hundred Boston men gathered at the Park Street

Church to hear Anthony Comstock, founder and secretary of the New York Society for the Suppression of Vice. No women were allowed because the planned "discussion was unfit for the delicate ears of Boston womanhood," according to Neil Miller, author of *Banned in Boston, the Watch and Ward Society's Crusade against Books, Burlesque and the Social Evil.*

Comstock was already a nationally famous crusader, obsessed with banning anything even vaguely sexual. "[A bad book] breeds lust. Lust defiles the body, debauches the imagination, corrupts the mind, deadens the will, destroys the memory, sears the conscience, hardens the heart, and damns the soul," he said. "It robs the soul of many virtues, and imprints upon the mind of youth, visions that throughout life curse the man or woman." In his first annual report in 1874, Comstock claimed to have seized 130,000 pounds of "bad" books and 194,000 "bad" pictures. The US postmaster general had given Comstock a special agent commission, and the 1873 Comstock Law gave the Postal Service the power to ban any items deemed lewd, lascivious, obscene, or of indecent character. "Comstockery" was a word coined by playwright George Bernard Shaw after Comstock called Shaw "an Irish smut dealer" because he had written a play about a prostitute.

"Comstockery became a term of ridicule, a synonym for Puritanism, censorship and general moral squeamishness," Miller wrote.

The Boston men that day heard Comstock brag about his success in cleansing New York City. Comstock told them he had also been instrumental in the recent arrest of sixteen men in Boston, and that thirteen of them had been convicted of selling obscene literature. He admitted he had entrapped a sixty-seven-year-old New York abortionist, Madame Restell, by posing as a man desperately broke who could not afford for his wife to have another child. Madame Restell was arrested when she sold him birth control materials and she subsequently slit her own throat while sitting in a bathtub. "A bloody end to a bloody life," Comstock shrugged.

Comstock noted there was much work to be done to cleanse Boston and the men in the audience enthusiastically agreed. They voted that day to form the New England Society for the Suppression of Vice. (Thirteen years later, they changed the title to the New England Watch and Ward Society, named after the Puritan police force that had patrolled the streets of Boston two centuries earlier.) Henry Chase, no relation to J. Franklin Chase, was appointed the first secretary and the Reverend Frederick B. Allen, who had established missions and social service agencies throughout the city, became president, a position he would hold for the next twenty-six years. The balance of the executive committee read like a who's who of Boston Blue Bloods—Unitarian minister Edward Everett Hale, preacher Philip Brooks, and philanthropist Robert Treat Paine among them.

"Frederick B. Allen," wrote Paul Boyer in his *Purity in Print,* "was a veritable Paul Bunyan of philanthropy.... The vice-society activists themselves had little doubt that they were acting as an 'enlightened civic conscience.' The Watch and Ward, proudly proclaiming itself a 'philanthropic association,' declared: 'While others endeavor to remedy the effects of crime, we strive to remove the causes. ... Every successful blow at immoral literature, the brothel, or the gambling hall goes far to remove the necessity for the hospital, the asylum, and the charity home.' ... To the few who challenged their activities on libertarian grounds, they merely offered the familiar reformist argument: 'Private interests must be subservient to the general interests of the community.'"

One of the first books the Watch and Ward went after was Walt Whitman's *Leaves of Grass,* which Boston publisher James Osgood had agreed to take on in 1881. Whitman's poems "To a Common Prostitute" and "A Woman Waits for Me" were just too erotic for the Blue Bloods and they impressed upon the district attorney to demand their complete removal. Whitman balked and had the book published in Philadelphia instead—the first edition sold out in one day.

By 1890, the Society had influenced the Massachusetts Legislature to pass a law making it illegal to publish or sell books or any other printed matter that was deemed to contain "obscene, indecent or impure language, or manifestly tending to the corruption of youth."

"The society finally had back the legal language that it required, setting the stage for years of battles to suppress books, magazines, and performances that it considered immoral," Miller wrote. "The Watch and Ward . . . would make the expression 'Banned in Boston' a national catchphrase."

"Banned in Boston" not only became a catchphrase, it also became a selling tool in other American cities. Being banned in Boston—as it had for *Leaves of Grass*—meant increased sales elsewhere. "The Boston fools have already made me more than $2,000," Whitman's Philadelphia publisher reportedly said.

Most Boston newspapers initially editorialized against the "narrow-minded tyranny and bigoted self-righteousness" of the Watch and Ward. In one of his annual addresses to the society, Allen responded, "We are simply trying to represent you, the thoughtful and pure-minded men and women of this community."

The Watch and Ward used "unofficial searchers and snoopers" and paid undercover investigators in Boston and other Massachusetts communities to ferret out faro games and other gambling activities, attend questionable plays and bawdy burlesque performances, and to purchase dirty pictures and books. The Watch and Ward also controversially hired college men to go into houses of ill repute to expose prostitution. The Watch and Ward did not have power to arrest, but had such a strong influence that judges invariably complied by issuing warrants for the police to execute.

By 1915 the Watch and Ward had been taking Boston's booksellers to court for decades for offering novels—including classics with slightly racy themes—that they deemed obscene. Booksellers who lost in court paid fines ranging from $100 to $1,000, and they finally cried "uncle." That year, the Society's J. Franklin Chase and Richard F. Fuller of the Old Corner Bookstore, set up the Boston Booksellers' Committee to avoid further prosecutions. Fuller, two other booksellers, and three Watch and Ward directors made up the committee. They read and evaluated current novels. If they all found a book acceptable, bookstores could sell it without fear of prosecution. If not, all Massachusetts book dealers were notified, and anyone selling the book would be a target for Watch and Ward action. Boston's newspapers agreed to refuse advertisements for the book or review it. If the committee members disagreed, the book was submitted to the district attorney or a magistrate for a tie-breaking decision.

"If the bookseller won't sell, and the reviewer won't review, the book might as well never have been written," Fuller proudly said.

The Watch and Ward's success in Boston also depended on another curious alliance of traditional enemies—the protestant Blue Bloods openly loathed the Roman Catholic Irish, but the Irish, through sheer numbers, now controlled Boston politics and its police force. The only thing they had in common was a fear of sexuality.

"Back of the Watch and Ward, then, stands the prestige of the Brahmins of the Commonwealth," Wood wrote, "and to it is added the vast influence of the Roman Catholic hierarchy, and the jury services of the Mc's and O's of South Boston and points West. 'The Irish make notable Puritans,' says the Rev. Mr. Chase."

Chase himself was an enigma—"tolerated, but hardly respected, by the cultivated residents of the Back Bay and the wealthier suburbs," according to Boyer. He was also tolerated but despised by the Irish whom he patronized. "He was a Pecksniff (a hypocritical Dickens character)," Mencken wrote.

Chase's partner in censorship was Watch and Ward treasurer Godfrey Lowell Cabot, possibly the wealthiest man in Boston, the bluest of Blue Bloods, and "very much a puritan," wrote Miller, "a man who clung to moral absolutes throughout his 101 years and who made a major part of his life's work the support of an organization devoted to stamping out even the mildest sexual references and innuendoes in books and on the stage." Imagine Cabot's family's surprise when his biographer, Leon Harris, five years after Cabot died in 1962, published lascivious letters Cabot had written to his wife while on business trips, including one from 1904 in which he said he had a dream that she urinated in his mouth and he "greedily" swallowed it.

As America roared into the 1920s, the Watch and Ward tried to pursue a less public course in guiding the Commonwealth's morals. During his stewardship, Chase helped bring 3,937 cases against houses of prostitution, booksellers, gamblers, theater owners, and dope dealers, and he had a 98 percent conviction rate. In many cases, the public was unaware of Watch and Ward involvement. One defense lawyer, a former district attorney who had worked with the Watch and Ward, called the society's paid snoopers "vicious little rats."

Comstock had died in 1915. By the 1920s, Comstockery became the punch line for jokes in New York, and Boston's curious arrangement—"the booksellers of Boston now appear to adore the censorship" Wood wrote—began to attract national notice.

Wood's sarcastic and biting "Keeping the Puritans Pure" in the September 1925 issue was the first salvo lobbed by Mencken in his *American Mercury* magazine.

"When a book has been condemned in Boston it stays condemned. There is no publicity," Wood wrote. "No avid young Bostonian with a lewd mind is informed that a volume to his liking may be bought by mail from an unregenerate New York publisher. Not a bubble comes to the surface to betray that some author's puppy has been tied in a bag and dropped in the Charles. . . . The pleasant scheme, that not only suppresses books but also suppresses all mention of those suppressed, permits the Rev. Mr. Chase to talk in his reports of 'waves of obscenity' and the good work of the Court of Preventive Criticism without the danger of having his tall talk contrasted with his short list."

Mencken wasn't done with the Boston "Pecksniff." Three months later in *American Mercury,* writer Charles Angoff attacked the Watch and Ward Society again, ripping into its Irish supporters whom he called "immigrant morons . . . multiplying like rabbits," who "have no more interest in ideas than a guinea pig has in Kant's *Critique of Pure Reason* or a donkey has in Goethe's *Faust.*"

Chase, always a brawler, was ready to get his revenge. In April 1926 he ordered the banning of that month's *American Mercury* magazine because it contained "Hatrack," a short story about a prostitute and hypocrisy in a small town in Missouri. Chase ruled the story obscene, even though it had no sexual references and just one "damned." (The same issue also included an article that named Chase as a "Methodist vice hunter of long practice.") A Harvard Square news dealer was arrested for selling the April issue to a Watch and Ward undercover agent. Mencken promptly got on a train in Baltimore, bound for Boston. To force the issue, he had agreed to personally sell Chase a copy of *American Mercury* at 2 p.m. on April 5 at Brimstone Corner, the aptly named intersection near Boston Common where the Watch and Ward had been started almost half a century earlier.

"More than a thousand curiosity seekers—largely Harvard undergraduates—turned out for the spectacle on the Common," Miller wrote. "Some hung off trees and out of windows. . . . Chase offered Mencken a silver half-dollar, and, in a theatrical moment that delighted the throng, the editor took the coin and bit the end of it to make sure it was genuine. Then he handed over a copy of the magazine. 'Officer, arrest that man,' commanded Chase."

Mencken was marched up Tremont Street to the Pemberton Square courthouse where he was booked on a charge of selling "certain obscene, indecent, and impure printing . . . manifestly tending to corrupt the morals of youth." The next day, though, as thousands vied to squeeze into the two-hundred-seat courtroom, Judge James Parmenter found Mencken not guilty and ruled that "Hatrack" contained "nothing that would arouse sexual impulses or lascivious thoughts."

"Mencken was free, he had beaten the Watch and Ward in its own bailiwick," Miller wrote. "It was a stunning verdict, not to mention a huge blemish on J. Frank's enviable string of convictions."

Across the Charles River in Cambridge that afternoon, a wild celebration ensued. At a luncheon in Harvard's student union, two thousand students and professors stood and gave Mencken a three-cheer ovation. He told them, "From now on we are going to make these fellows bring their charges into the open. And they are easy to beat. When you go after them, ninety-nine percent will run, and the other one percent is easy pickings."

It was all downhill for Frank Chase after that. Even the Boston newspapers that had supported him turned against him. The *Boston Herald* criticized him in an editorial—"a censor should be sure he has a case." The Boston Police commissioner banned further stunt arrests. Will Rogers, in his nationally syndicated column, described Chase and the Watch and Ward as "the Ku Kluxers of Boston literature." The Irish-leaning *Boston Telegram* ran a series exposing the methods of Chase and the Watch and Ward with headlines "Pretty College Girls Used as Lures" and "Watch and Ward Thugs Cover Up Back Bay 'Love Nests' of Rich Men." A *Telegram* editorial said: "Chase stands discredited . . . he has shamed all the sincere, honest and upright crusaders against vice. . . . He is through as a fake reformer." The Brahmin's favorite newspaper, the *Transcript,* called Chase and the Society "sanctimonious . . . semi-official meddlers." The Watch and Ward Society board blamed everything on Chase.

"Richard F. Fuller completely turned against his erstwhile colleague," Boyer wrote. "'Chase is licked—bungled the job—made a damned fool of himself,' he told a Knopf salesman."

It got worse for Chase. In October, six months after the trial, Mencken's lawyers filed a $50,000 suit in federal court against Chase and the Watch and Ward Society charging them with interfering with Mencken's magazine. Without Chase's approval, Fuller and the Watch and Ward lawyers, in exchange for the suit being dropped, quickly agreed to quit using Chase's "gentleman's agreement" and promised to do any future book banning in the public eye.

All that was too much for Chase. He fell ill with pneumonia and on November 3, 1926, he died. His friend Delcevare King, who had convinced him to take the Watch and Ward job nineteen years earlier, wrote a letter to the *Herald* saying Chase was an unappreciated "hero." Mencken, never one to mince words, wrote: "Now he

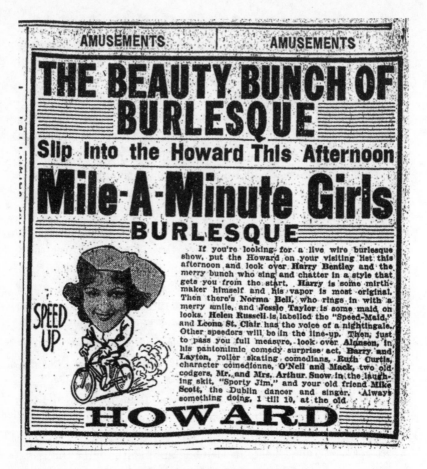

1918 NEWSPAPER AD FOR THE OLD HOWARD THEATRE

was dead at last in defeat and dismay, and we were rid of him . . . I am told that worry over the case, especially over the reprisals we held over him, helped to kill him. I hope so."

The Watch and Ward Society, greatly weakened, staggered on until 1957—one of its final successes was harassing the world-famous Old Howard burlesque theater into closing in 1953—but it never regained the power it had in the J. Franklin Chase era. Book censorship in Boston continued, but after 1926 it became a free-for-all with the Watch and Ward Society, various ministers, the police, district attorney, and the Catholic Church all choosing their own books to suppress. More than seventy books, including Hemingway's *The Sun Also Rises,* Theodore Dreiser's *An American Tragedy,* Upton Sinclair's *Oil!,* and Sinclair Lewis's *Elmer Gantry,* were banned in Boston in 1927 alone. By then, the Boston prudes had become a national joke. Authors and publishers reveled in the book-banning frenzy because, even though Bostonians bought more books per capita than residents of any other city, "Banned in Boston" rang cash registers everywhere else.

"Boston," Upton Sinclair said, "is our advertising department."

CHAPTER 11

James Michael Curley
"Like all demagogues, he exploited a real need"

Even today in Boston, more than a half century after his death, the name James Michael Curley elicits equal responses of "What a crook!" and "What a saint!"

The saint response comes from the descendants of the famine Irish, who journeyed under Curley's patronage from a despised Boston minority to the Hub's powerful majority.

The crook response comes from most everyone else, especially the descendants of the Boston Blue Bloods, whom Curley delighted in attacking from the time he first ran for an alderman seat in 1898 until his tenth and final run for mayor in 1955.

"Repeatedly during his long career of public service and demagoguery, Curley would so irritate Bostonians and other Bay Staters that they would clamp him down in the oblivion of private life," Reinhard H. Luthin and Allan Nevins wrote in their 1954 book, *American Demagogues: Twentieth Century.* "But, like some annoying Jack-in-the-Box, he would always unloose himself and bob up again . . . One commentator, after a Curley election victory, observed: 'Bostonians have again disproved the charge that they are narrow-minded people. They can see merits in James M. Curley not visible to anyone else.'"

Whenever the opportunity arose, Curley derided the Brahmins and their most prestigious institutions, including Harvard College, with much political gain among his Irish Catholic supporters. The "Mayor of the Poor" (alternately known as the "Jailbird Mayor of Boston") once wrote to a member of the Harvard Board of Overseers, "The Massachusetts of the Puritans is as dead as Caesar, but there is no need to mourn the fact. Their successors—the Irish—had letters and learning, culture and civilization when the ancestors of the Puritans were savages running half-naked through the forests of Britain. It took the Irish to make Massachusetts a fit place to live in."

Although he was often a progressive mayor, governor, and congressman, Curley was also undoubtedly a crook. He served two prison terms for fraud and he siphoned so much public money into his own pockets that he became the national poster boy for political corruption.

He was as Irish as a shamrock but he always played by his own rules, even against other Irishmen. John F. "Honey" Fitzgerald, the grandfather of President John F. Kennedy, learned that the hard way. Curley blackmailed then Mayor "Honey Fitz" into abandoning his quest for reelection in 1913 by threatening to reveal the mayor's involvement with Toodles, a voluptuous twenty-three-year-old cigarette girl.

Curley's life began in Boston in 1874, although in many ways it began between 1845 and 1849 when the great potato famine drove tens of thousands of Ireland's sons and daughters to Boston, joining an already swelling Gaelic population in Massachusetts. The Irish in America were poor, uneducated, hated, and misused. By the 1850s, "Irish Need Not Apply" signs hung on factory doors in the Hub, and Protestant politicians sponsored anti-immigration legislation—under a "pauper removal law" 1,300 of the most desperate Irish in Boston were even shipped back to Liverpool. The Irish in Boston, almost to a man, joined the antireform, anti-abolition Democratic Party. Their numbers grew—the Irish were the ethnic majority in the Hub by 1880—but the Yankees and their money still controlled business, government, and the press. Most of the Irish in Boston lived in poorer enclaves in Southie, Roxbury, and Dorchester well into the twentieth century, and they had a smoldering community resentment of blacks. "Boston had stood for progress in religion and politics; now it was home to [Catholics] whose official organ, *The Pilot,* called the sacred cause of abolition 'niggerology' and Lincoln a 'boob,'" Jack Beatty wrote in his biography, *The Rascal King.*

James Michael Curley

Curley's parents, Michael and Sarah, both emigrated from Galway in 1864, married in 1870, and settled in Roxbury's Ward 17, a rough neighborhood of tenements. Sarah gave birth to three sons—John, then James, then Michael, who died at two years old. Curley's thirty-four-year-old father died three years later after picking up a huge stone while working as a laborer.

Curley came by his dishonesty honestly. He watched his young widowed mother wear her knees raw scrubbing the floors of the rich, and it fueled in him the resentment that defined Boston politics for almost half a century. Curley clawed his way out of the slums of Ward 17, using his fists and favors, his wit and his tongue; his life mirrored the Boston Irish experience—clannish and familial, Catholic and fatalistic.

In 1897 at twenty-three years old, he borrowed money to buy a coat and vest at a store that sold the used clothing of Harvard students, and then ran for the Ward 17 seat on the Boston Common Council. He narrowly lost. He lost again in 1898, but finally won in 1899. About that time, he and a friend formed a Ward 17 social and political organization they called the Tammany Club after the scandal-ridden New York City administration. It would soon prove an entirely appropriate name with Curley as the club's perennial president.

"Prominent Ward 17 Democratic Politicians Suspected of Fraud by Federal Officers," screamed a front-page headline in the *Boston Herald* on February 11, 1903. Curley, by then a state representative, and a fellow politician had taken the civil service test for two recent Irish immigrants who wanted to be postmen. They had been recognized and all four were jailed. Curley admitted during the trial that he had taken the test and used for the first time the phrase that would get him elected over and over. "I did it for a friend," he said, for a man who needed the job to feed his wife and kids.

Curley ran a campaign for alderman from his jail cell and won a seat on the 1904 board while incarcerated. Distributing favors and jobs to friends and Christmas gifts to Ward 17 children, he easily won a seat as an alderman/city councillor every year after that until 1911. Curley was already playing his "us-against-them" card at every opportunity.

"Between 1900 and 1914, Curley bred unprecedented tumult in Boston politics," Beatty wrote. "He was denounced from pulpits and excoriated by editorialists. Headlines made his name synonymous with scandal. His 'image,' as we would call his reputation today, would never be cleansed of this early taint. And yet without it his political ascent would not have been possible. For every enemy bad publicity made him, it made him two friends."

Curley's opponents were most often the Boston Brahmins, the affluent Protestant scions of the Puritans. The Irish Catholics hated them and they hated the Irish Catholics. "In this mutual dislike, the ingenious leader of Ward 17 saw political possibilities," Luthin and Nevins wrote. "He developed into an indefatigable baiter of the Brahmins, now in the minority. 'Jim,' remarked one student of the Boston scene, 'can make the term blue blood sound like the vilest epithet known to man.'"

Curley learned early that as long as he could keep his followers focused on that class war, he could do pretty much whatever he wanted to. While he glibly derided the Bradfords and Bacons, the Cabots and Choates, the Lodges, the Lowells, and the Saltonstalls, he filled his own pockets with ill-gotten cash.

Curley railed against immigration restrictions when he went to Washington following his election to Congress in 1911, earning him new friends among Massachusetts's burgeoning Italian and Jewish populations. His sights were set on becoming mayor, though, and when Mayor John F. "Honey" Fitzgerald announced he wouldn't run for reelection in 1913, Curley threw his fedora into the ring along with eight other candidates. Seven of Boston's nine daily newspapers promptly editorialized against him.

Honey Fitz briefly reentered the campaign, but threats by Curley to reveal Fitzgerald's involvement with twenty-three-year-old Elizabeth "Toodles" Ryan forced Honey Fitz out of the race. (Curley had even placed a notice in newspapers of a lecture series he planned that included "Libertines in History from Henry the

Eighth to the Present Day" and "Great Lovers from Cleopatra to Toodles.") In the finals, Curley faced Thomas Kenny of South Boston, also an Irishman but the candidate of the Yankee-controlled Good Government Association, or "Goo Goos" as Curley called them. "There has been no man in my experience on the city government who has shown less capacity and whose record in public life is more questionable than that of Mr. Curley," Kenny, a respected lawyer, commented.

Curley beat Kenny by less than 6,000 votes of the 80,000 cast, and the era of the Purple Shamrock began. He lost in 1917—although he kept Honey Fitz out of that race simply by suggesting he still might give his "Great Lovers" lecture—but won again in 1921, 1929, and 1945. In between his mayoral stints, he served as president of the Hibernia Savings Bank, as governor from 1935 to 1937, and as congressman again from 1943 to 1947.

While mayor, he ran up deficits and drove the wealthy to the suburbs with tax increases by undertaking huge public building projects, personally negotiating the contracts—and always taking his chunk. After his death, Boston turned his twenty-one-room mansion in Jamaica Plain, with its marble fireplace and shamrocks carved into all of the window shutters, into a historical landmark. The joke in the Hub back then was that it was the second time the city had paid for the house.

Curley handed out government jobs to his family and friends, qualifications be damned. When he became governor in 1935, he appointed a grocery salesman to be Commissioner of Agriculture. He tried to appoint Margaret O'Riordan as State Librarian but was turned down by the Governor's Council after reporters interviewed her and she told them the only things she ever read were *Spy Stories* and *True Romance* magazines.

As mayor, Curley ended the corruption of the ward bosses—but he did it by taking their patronage under his personal control. He met with needy constituents every day, finding them jobs or helping them with creditors or police problems—and thus grew an army of friends who owed him favors and votes. Even as a middle-aged man, he was quick with his fists when words failed, which wasn't often since he had, as the Irish say, "the gift of gab." He made thousands of friends and thousands of enemies. He was larger than life, so much so that a fictional character based on him, Frank Skeffington, the protagonist of the best-selling novel, *The Last Hurrah*—published and made into a hit film while Curley was still alive—is often confused with the real man.

His triumphs were matched by his tragedies. His first wife, Mary Herlihy Curley, suffered a lingering death from cancer in 1930—"Mayor Curley's devotion to his wife made even his enemies admire him," the *Boston Herald* opined—and six months later an embolism killed his twenty-three-year-old heir apparent, James Michael Jr. By 1944 five of his nine children had died—twins John and Joseph in infancy, Dorothea at fourteen from pneumonia, and son Paul, a hopeless alcoholic, who passed in his sleep at thirty-two. But nothing could have prepared Curley for February 11, 1950—a month after his final mayoral term ended—when his forty-one-year-old daughter Mary and thirty-four-year-old son Leo both suffered cerebral hemorrhages just hours apart while talking on the same phone in the same apartment on Beacon Street.

"No matter what you say of him, you have to admire him for his great courage," John F. Kennedy, then a thirty-three-year-old congressman, said to a friend as they left the dual wake in Curley's Jamaica Plain home on February 12. Political grudges are seldom forgiven in Boston, but they took a backseat that day. The seventy-five-year-old Curley stood beside his son's and daughter's caskets—Mary laid out in a white party dress and Leo in his Naval officer's uniform—greeting the estimated fifty thousand people who came from around the city and state. The mourners included Archbishop Richard Cushing, Boston Pops Conductor Arthur Fiedler, old political rivals, schoolchildren, and cleaning women.

Those cleaning women, along with teamsters, laborers, dockworkers, widows, and waitresses, had been his base. Curley had become the champion of the immigrant and second-generation Irish—and also of the newly arrived Italians, Jews, and other poor Europeans—by continuously fighting his class war with the Brahmins for more than half a century. In speech after speech, Curley recalled his people's persecution by the Know Nothings in 1850s Boston, when the famine Irish were treated as less than human—"leeches" according to one Know Nothing newspaper— and the majority of the deaths in Boston's Irish ghettos were children under five. Things did get better for the Irish in the twentieth century, but Curley made sure the resentment never went away.

Curley claimed it was the Irish who made Boston a great city, and with a wink—everything was always with a wink—said the Boston Tea Party was really the Boston Beer Party, conceived in a tavern owned by an Irishman. He continued to use "blue blood" as a curse in his many us-against-them speeches delivered in a voice described by Beatty as "smooth and rich and it had extraordinary range; in a single sentence, he could shift from baritone to tenor to countertenor."

While in office, Curley awarded contracts willy-nilly, often with no way to pay for them, but always with a piece for himself. Boston businessmen complained about the soaring taxes, and Curley often found it necessary to borrow money to meet the city's bills and pay salaries. The city's Finance Commission once attempted to examine the mayor's contracts—and even accused him of political favoritism—but he was handing out so many contracts the commission fell hopelessly behind in its investigation.

"When one bank president refused his request for a loan to the city, Curley warned him over the telephone: 'Listen! There's a water main with floodgates right under your building. You'd better get that money up by three o'clock this afternoon, or those gates will be opened, pouring thousands of gallons of water right into your vaults,'" Luthin and Nevins wrote. "The bank president, cowed, put the money on the line."

Curley whipped up resentment whenever he had the chance, appealing to religious as well as class antagonisms. Once, while giving a speech to an Irish-American audience in Southie, he closed with, "And where was my esteemed opponent when all this was going on? He was in the Ritz Hotel in white tie and tails eating a steak dinner—and on a Friday!"

In a speech in the Italian North End, Curley said, "Republicans don't want someone to care for babies, the aged and to pay a living wage. They want someone who will sit on the lid, will not spend and will cut down debt. Government was not created to save money and to cut debt but to take care of people. That's my theory of government."

Curley did take care of people—especially himself. "Everybody knew," biographer Joseph Dinneen wrote, "there wasn't a contract awarded that did not carry with it a cut for Curley." He took long vacations in first-class hotels, sent his kids to private schools, bought a yacht, and left big tips. "In this way he spent hundreds of thousands of dollars, much of which he did not earn but took, indirectly, from the working- and lower-middle-class taxpayers of Boston," Beatty wrote. "Yet he said that the title he cherished most was 'the Mayor of the Poor,' and the poor venerated him."

Between 1898 and 1955, Curley ran for office thirty-two times. He served on the Boston City Council and on its predecessors, the Boston Common Council and Board of Aldermen. He was elected to the Massachusetts House of Representatives for one term. He won all but one of his five Congressional races. He ran for mayor ten times and won four terms. His last term, 1946–1949, included five months in a federal penitentiary. He ran for governor three times, winning once in 1934, and ran unsuccessfully for the US Senate in 1936 when he glibly called Henry Cabot Lodge Jr., his Brahmin opponent, "Little Boy Blue."

Curley died from stomach cancer in 1958. Beatty wrote that after a five-hour operation, Curley momentarily opened his eyes, saw reporters and his son Francis there, and, with a wink, said, "Franno, I wish to announce the first plank in my campaign for reelection—we're going to have the floors in this goddamned hospital smoothed out."

Those were his last words. More than one hundred thousand people attended his wake at the State House—including the scrubwomen to whom he had provided long-handled mops while governor to get them off their knees. An estimated one million people lined the streets for his funeral procession.

Love him or hate him, there was no middle ground. In a 1984 essay historian Charles Trout argued that Curley never received his due as a great progressive. Lost in his habit of slipping public money into his own pocket, his inauguration threat to sell Boston Common, and his quips about the Brahmins tracing family lineage that could "easily have proven that they sailed with Captain Kidd or with some other man equally honest," there lived a true reformer, Trout wrote. In addition to initiating public projects that included vocational high schools, bridges, tunnels, beaches, and roads, Curley advocated pensions for city workers and the creation of a statewide old-age assistance program. He supported better benefits for government workers and the labor unions. He demanded mentally disabled patients in the Fernald School be given pillows. He fought to maintain the nickel fare on all streetcars and subways, and he opposed construction of elevated train lines as a noisy blight on neighborhoods. He became more and more reckless with taking his cuts and helping his cronies over the years, however, and "more given to demagogic appeals," as Trout put it. He never won a statewide election other than the gubernatorial contest in 1934 during the depths of the Great Depression.

In 1947 during his last term as mayor and still holding his seat in Congress, the seventy-two-year-old Curley was jailed again—this time in the federal penitentiary in Danbury, Connecticut, for mail fraud—until President Harry Truman commuted the sentence and later gave him a complete pardon. He was welcomed back to Boston like a conquering hero, but promptly made a new enemy when he claimed he did more work in his first five days back than his stand-in, John B. Hynes, did in five months. Hynes, who had actually done all the work, wouldn't forgive him for that slight and narrowly beat Curley in the next mayoral election. Curley challenged him again in 1951 and lost.

"Any number of progressives and, later, liberal Democrats thought him tainted," Trout wrote. "He would forever be the 'Jailbird Mayor of Boston' . . . By the end of his life, he had retreated into the identity picked up by [author] Edwin O'Connor in *The Last Hurrah,* a portrait that does not do him justice."

Curley had become by 1954 a national punch line to any joke about cronyism and official corruption. Many Brahmins had become Democrats by then, and many of Irish heritage had bettered their lot and moved to the suburbs. Some had even become Republicans. Bostonians enjoyed reminiscing about Curley, but they also felt embarrassment. Curley, at eighty-one years old and crushed by the weight of his own legacy, ran half-heartedly once more in 1955 but lost in the primary. Three years later, the Mayor of the Poor died and he had a true last hurrah when throngs of adoring Bostonians came to the statehouse to pay their respects.

"James Michael Curley was a prototype of the urban demagogue who exploited religious and class insecurity for his own political advantage," Luthin and Nevins wrote. "One cannot blame the downtrodden minorities of America's cities if they seek a champion—even one of doubtful quality. If racial, religious and social prejudice did not exist—if the proper Bostonians had cared more for those less proper—Curley might never have risen to power. Like all demagogues, he exploited a real need, a real fear, a real hatred. Boston's Irish did not care if he was dishonest, if he served time in a state or federal penitentiary. He brought color and prestige into their lives; he attacked the 'blue bloods.' That was enough for them."

CHAPTER 12

Arthur P. Jell
"A tremendous calamity . . . treated with the utmost indifference"

The great black mass didn't adhere to the cliché, "as slow as molasses." Instead, the fifteen-foot-high wave unleashed by the collapse of a tank in the North End of Boston on January 15, 1919, surged at thirty-five miles an hour.

The 2.3-million-gallon flood of molasses, spreading in all directions, crushed and drowned everything in its path—people, horses, and other animals. The fast-moving tidal wave picked up trucks and railroad cars, crushed wood-frame homes into splinters, and filled their cellar holes with black gunk. The molasses picked a fire station up off its foundation and tipped it over. It colored the blue-green sea water a deep brown as it rolled into Boston Harbor. A section of the collapsed fifty-eight-foot-high United States Industrial Alcohol (USIA) tank sliced through and toppled the elevated trolley line, and only the quick actions of the brakeman on a train that had just passed averted the crash of another.

Reporters from Boston's daily newspapers and rescue workers, including more than one hundred sailors from the USS *Nantucket* and *Bessie J.* docked nearby, rushed to the scene.

"Molasses, waist deep, covered the street and swirled and bubbled about the wreckage," reported the *Boston Post*. "Here and there struggled a form—whether it was an animal or human being it was impossible to tell. Only an upheaval, a thrashing about in the sticky mess, showed where any life was. . . . Horses died like so many flies on sticky flypaper. The more they struggled, the deeper in the mess they were ensnared. Human beings—men and women—suffered likewise."

Twenty-one people died in what came to be called the Great Boston Molasses Disaster, and more than 1,500 were injured, many in ways they would never recover from, physically or mentally. Two of the dead were Pasquale Iantosca and Maria Destasio, both ten years old, who had been playing near the tank. When the resulting class action lawsuit was before the court, lawyers for USIA argued that Pasquale and Maria's families should not receive any damages because the children were trespassing on company property.

That "public be damned" attitude had marked USIA's history in Boston, from the location of the fifty-eight-foot high and ninety-foot wide monstrosity in the heavily populated neighborhood, to the tank's shoddy construction and maintenance, and to the company's baseless defense that the tank had not collapsed but instead had been blown up by anarchists.

"It was a tremendous calamity which would appeal to everything that is human in mankind, yet was treated with the utmost indifference by the defendant," Damon Hall, lead attorney for the plaintiffs, would later say.

No one was more indifferent than Arthur P. Jell, the ambitious USIA treasurer, who—despite no background in engineering— had approved the plans for the tank, cut corners on the thickness of its steel, rushed the construction in 1915, skipped a crucial test before the tank was initially filled, and refused to heed warnings even from his own employees that the tank was unsafe and failing. When everyone in the North End noticed the tank was leaking— children including Maria and Pasquale would actually bring pails to fill with the sticky sweet goo—Jell ordered the tank caulked. When the leaks continued, he ordered the tank painted brown so the dripping syrup wouldn't be so obvious.

When employee Isaac Gonzales brought rusty shards as evidence that the tank might be failing to Jell's USIA office in East Cambridge, the treasurer was upset that the man's boots had muddied his carpet. "I don't know what you want me to do," Jell said. "The tank still stands." He then threatened to fire Gonzales if he continued to raise red flags.

When Jell arrived on the scene one hour after the collapse—a scene described by many as more horrific than any battlefield in just-ended World War I—his first thoughts were not for the dead and dying, nor the dozens of victims still trapped in the molasses and wreckage, not even for the many stuck horses who were screaming and being shot in the head to end their sufferings. His only thoughts—and those of his superiors at USIA headquarters in New York—were to avoid liability.

"His bosses had instructed him to remain silent, to let the company attorney, [Henry] Dolan, issue any statements about the disaster, and, above all, to ensure that no city inspector or law enforcement officials confiscate USIA property—specifically pieces of the tank," wrote Stephen Puleo in *Dark Tide: The Great Boston Molasses Flood of 1919*. Although the tank only stood on the edge of Boston Harbor from late 1915 to early 1919, its construction and collapse provides "a microcosm of America," according to Puleo. The North End had long been one of the most heavily populated areas of Boston—Paul Revere and hated royal Governor Thomas Hutchinson both called the North End home, as did the masses of Irish immigrants who lived there cheek to jowl in tenements beginning in the mid-nineteenth century. By the early 1900s, Italians, especially the unschooled and unskilled from southern Italy, had replaced most of the Irish who had moved on to South Boston, Charlestown, and other areas of the city. The Italians also replaced the Irish as the vilified object of the Boston Brahmins' prejudice.

"Southern Italians are apt to be ignorant, lazy, destitute and superstitious," Henry Cabot Lodge, Massachusetts's Republican US Senator and founder of the Immigration Restriction League, said. "In addition, a considerable percentage of those from cities are criminals."

The Italians in the North End were defenseless when Jell decided to construct his tank there. Most were not politically active—those who were involved in matters beyond *la famiglia* tended to be anarchists—and most didn't even speak English. The anarchists were particularly hated and feared by Americans because the most radical of them advocated violence against big business and the government, and their random bombings killed innocent people. In 1916 anarchists exploded a bomb at the North End's Salutation Street police station and attempted to explode one at a USIA plant in Brooklyn, New York. No one was injured in either incident. The USIA plant was targeted because USIA distilled molasses into industrial alcohol, which was used in the manufacture of munitions sold to the allies fighting in Europe. Anarchists were opposed to the war and once the United States entered it in 1917, many—including Nicola Sacco and Bartolomeo Vanzetti—brought further enmity on their movement by becoming draft dodgers, commonly called "slackers" in that era.

Even before the United States entered the fray, the war helped business boom for United States Industrial Alcohol. In 1914 thirty-five-year-old Jell was put in charge of expanding its capacity in USIA's Boston operation—a subsidiary called Purity Distilling.

With no political pressure to contend with—and despite its dense population and proximity to a hotbed of anarchism—Jell decided the North End would be the perfect place for the construction of a 2.3-million-gallon tank. The property, just two hundred feet from inner Boston Harbor on Commercial Street, would allow freighters from the West Indies, Puerto Rico, and Cuba easy access to off-load their molasses. Tank cars on the Boston and Worcester Railroad could then easily transport the molasses to Purity/ USIA's distillation plant in East Cambridge.

Jell ran into multiple problems, though, in negotiating with the Boston Elevated Railway Company to lease the property, which is next to the present-day US Coast Guard base. In October, Jell wrote to the contractors, the Hammond Iron Works, that the lease would begin on November 1 and that, "we are extremely anxious to have the work proceed as rapidly as possible and are quite willing to pay any additional expenses there may be in pushing the work forward so that the tank can be completed promptly." In a second letter, Jell confirmed USIA would pay any additional expenses to "hurry the work" so that it would be completed by December 15.

Jell also assured Hammond no permits would be needed because the tank would be considered a "receptacle" and not a building. By early December, Jell was particularly eager to have the tank finished because a USIA tanker filled with molasses was already steaming north from Cuba, and if the Boston tank was not ready, the tanker would have to travel to another USIA site and unload its cargo for storage there. If Jell, who had first arrived in Boston as Purity's secretary in 1909, succeeded in this task, a USIA vice presidency and move to company headquarters in New York was assured.

"When [USIA president Frederic] Harrison ordered him to begin work on the Boston tank project, there was more than a veiled implication that his success on this project would expedite his promotion and failure would doom his future with the company," Puleo wrote.

As Hammond rushed to finish the tank, and as the USIA tanker steamed north, Jell made two fatal decisions. One is that he approved using steel that was significantly thinner than what was called for in the specifications of the curved plates that formed the tank. The construction specifications also called for the tank to be tested by filling it with water. Jell decided to forego that test, saving money on the cost of water and, more importantly, time. Instead, he ordered Hammond to fill it only up to six inches, covering the first angle joints. When no leak occurred, Jell was satisfied the tank was sound and ready. The tanker arrived on December 31, 1915, and off-loaded 700,000 gallons into the tank. A month later, Jell wrote a letter to Hammond thanking them for "the manner in which you rushed this work."

The tank immediately exhibited problems.

"From the beginning leaks had appeared," Chuck Lyons wrote in "A Sticky Tragedy" in *History Today* magazine. "Streaks of molasses ran down the sides of the tank, and people living nearby filled up cans for home use. Children would scrape the leaks onto

Workers stand in molasses near a section of the tank.

COURTESY OF THE BOSTON PUBLIC LIBRARY, LESLIE JONES COLLECTION

sticks to make molasses suckers. Neighbors and workmen had also reported ominous rumbling noises inside the structure."

Despite the warnings, and with the war business booming, the tank was refilled to its 2.3-million-gallon capacity seven times in the next three years.

In April 1917, President Woodrow Wilson abandoned his efforts to keep the United States out of World War I and declared war on Germany. The US troops and munitions proved the difference, and after a year and a half more of warfare horrors unlike any before, Germany surrendered on November 11, 1918. The doughboys returned home, but it was to a new America. Anarchists had stepped up their violence. Unions were flexing their muscles, and labor unrest included a Boston Police strike. A 1918 flu epidemic that claimed millions of lives worldwide had not spared Massachusetts, and circus-sized tents were used to cover hundreds of coffins in some cemeteries when the ground was too frozen to dig graves.

Also, the century-long battle over demon rum had come to a head in the United States, and the supporters of temperance were winning. By 1919, states were lining up to support the eighteenth amendment to the Constitution. Prohibition became a certainty, although a provision in the law would put off implementation for a year.

In that grace period, Jell saw an opening. He and other USIA officials decided to refit the East Cambridge plant to manufacture grain alcohol instead of industrial alcohol. If they could do it quickly, they would have time to supply rum makers before Prohibition became the law of the land. On January 13, 1919, a USIA ship, the *Miliero,* off-loaded 1.3 million gallons of warm molasses into the North End tank, already almost half-filled with molasses nearly frozen. On January 15, the outside temperature in Boston rose to an unseasonably warm forty degrees. The molasses in the leaking tank began making even louder rumbling and bubbling noises than usual.

"Inside the Boston and Worcester freight terminal, Percy Smerage . . . had just told his assistant to finish loading the last car when a low, deep rumble shook the freight yard," John Mason wrote in *Yankee Magazine* in 1965. "Then the earth heaved under their feet and they heard a sound of ripping and tearing—snipping of steel bolts (like a machine gun)—followed by a booming roar as the bottom of the giant molasses tank split wide open and a geyser of yellowish-brown fluid spouted into the sky, followed by a tidal wave of molasses. With a horrible, hissing, sucking sound, it splashed in a curving arc straight across the street, crushing everything and everybody in its path."

Even before the black wave of death had stopped moving, Jell and the USIA lawyers were conjuring excuses to avoid responsibility. City officials helped them—Mayor Andrew Peters stood in shin-deep molasses at the scene and called the collapse the result of an "explosion." USIA lawyer Henry F. R. Dolan issued a statement saying the tank's collapse was caused by "outside influences. . . . We know beyond question that the tank was not weak . . . we know, and our experts feel satisfied, that there was no fermentation because the molasses was not of sufficient temperature to ferment."

Eleven of the dead were found before nightfall, the other ten in the days to come. The last found was thirty-seven-year-old truck driver Flaminio Gallerani who, along with his four-ton lorry, was carried into Boston Harbor on the wave of molasses. His body was pulled from beneath a pier on January 27. "Luckily," Puleo wrote, "only his hands were eaten by sea animals," making it possible for his nephew to identify the body.

The cleanup took weeks; salty seawater blasted through fire hoses was used to finally dislodge the hardening mess. Although Dolan continued to insist that "evilly disposed persons," had blown up the tank, others, including state chemist Walter Wedger and US Inspector of Explosives Daniel T. O'Connell, pointed out that area windows had not shattered, as they would have if there had been an explosion, and they believed the tank collapsed because of structural weakness and fermentation.

That argument would continue for years. Before February was out, Superior Criminal Court Justice Wilfred Bolster had ruled the disaster was solely the fault of USIA and faulty tank construction. MIT professor C. M. Spofford tested the steel used in the tank's plates and found it was of "insufficient thickness." Although a grand jury declined to indict anyone for manslaughter—and Arthur Jell in December 1919 received his coveted promotion and moved to New York—the Boston Molasses Disaster case was far from over.

some things don't change

One hundred and twenty-five civil lawsuits were filed against the United States Industrial Alcohol Company. The suits were combined, and World War I hero Hugh W. Ogden, who had served as Judge Advocate in the famous Rainbow Division in France, was appointed to act as auditor and hear the evidence. The hearing, originally slated for six weeks, would become the longest in Massachusetts's history, and it would be six years before Ogden made his special report.

"There were so many lawyers involved, that there wasn't room enough in the courthouse to hold them all, so they consolidated and chose two to represent the claimants," Mason wrote. "Never in New England did so many engineers, metallurgists and scientists parade onto the witness stand. Albert L. Colby, an authority on the amount of structural strain a steel tank could sustain before breaking, was on the witness stand three weeks—often giving testimony as late as ten o'clock in the evening. Altogether, more than 3,000 witnesses were examined and nearly 45,000 pages of testimony and arguments were recorded. The defendants spent over $50,000 on expert witness fees, claiming the collapse was not due to a structural weakness but rather to a dynamite bomb.'"

USIA's lead lawyer Charles Choate continuously tried to play the anarchist angle, even producing a witness who claimed she saw a puff of smoke coming from the top of the tank just before it collapsed. Many believed Choate's "outside agent" theory—the nation had just been through a Red Scare when "anarchists and Bolsheviks" had attempted to assassinate prominent government and business leaders. On September 16, 1920, Mike Boda, aka Mario Buda, an associate of Sacco and Vanzetti, had detonated a bomb on Wall Street that killed thirty-eight innocent people and injured more than two hundred others. Still, Damon Hall, the plaintiffs' lead lawyer, scoffed at the claim that "a mythical anarchist," at midday on the busy waterfront, had somehow climbed undetected to the top of the tank and dropped dynamite through an air vent.

Choate tried to prevent Jell from testifying, claiming that his testimony would not be relevant to the case. Ogden disagreed, but did allow Jell to give his deposition in March 1921 in New York instead of enduring what Choate called the "immense inconvenience" of traveling to Boston. Upon his arrival at New York's Belmont Hotel, Hall immediately ripped into Jell, establishing that he had no engineering background or expertise, and that he had ignored the "factor of safety" when he allowed thinner steel to be used than what the plans specified. Jell conceded that he had rushed construction, that no qualified person had ever reviewed the plans for safety, that delays had caused USIA "embarrassment," and that he had skipped the water test because the arrival of a tanker full of molasses was imminent. "Are there any other reasons why the water test was not made?" Hall asked. "It was considered an unnecessary expense," Jell replied, and when Hall questioned by whom, he said, "By me."

In his closing arguments two and a half years later, Hall ripped into the defense for successfully keeping Jell out of Ogden's courtroom. "Now I don't blame them for that attitude, because the story you get from Jell was, as I have said and repeated, one of the most sordid stories that it is possible to imagine, where everything was sacrificed for money."

Ogden agreed in a fifty-one-page report that he completed on April 28, 1925. He found the defendants responsible for the disaster and "reserved his harshest criticism for Arthur P. Jell and the USIA management that allowed him to oversee the project," according to Puleo. Ogden was particularly incensed that Jell had ignored the warnings of Isaac Gonzales and the telltale leaks on the tank. Ogden recommended about $300,000 ($30 million in today's dollars) in damages, including an estimated $6,000 to the estates of each victim. When Hall said he would seek more from a jury, Choate negotiated, and within hours USIA agreed to more than double the damages.

Jell, who did not attend any of the hearings in Boston, continued to work for USIA in New York. He later moved to Maryland and died at age eighty-five in 1963.

Puleo calls it a "folksy myth recounted by cab drivers and citizens alike that on hot summer days, for years after the flood, one could still smell the sweet, sticky aroma of molasses." Others still insist that it is true, and not just an urban legend. "One could discern throughout much of downtown Boston, and especially around the North End, the unmistakable aroma of molasses," Edwards Park recalled in *Smithsonian* magazine in 1983. "As a boy, I never questioned that odor, so strong on hot days, so far-reaching when the wind came out of the east. It was simply part of Boston, along with the Swan Boats in the Public Gardens and the tough kids swimming in the Frog Pond on the Common."

CHAPTER 13

Harry Frazee
"The name is mud in Boston"

In the lingo of kids today, Harry H. Frazee was a hater.

A Boston hater.

"The best thing about Boston was the train ride back to New York," the Broadway producer once said. Unfortunately, for Hub sports fans, Boston hater Frazee owned the Boston Red Sox from 1916 to 1923, and on January 5, 1920, strapped for cash to finance his play *My Lady Friends* (later revived as a musical, *No, No, Nanette*), he sold the great Babe Ruth to the New York Yankees for $125,000 and a $350,000 mortgage on Fenway Park.

That sale would come to be called, "The Curse of the Bambino." Led by the Babe, the Yankees won their first World Series title in 1923 and added three more championships during the Sultan of Swat's storied career.

The Red Sox, who had won the Series in 1918, would play eighty-six more years—literally a lifetime, a long lifetime—before winning another in 2004. Not only did the Red Sox not win in the decades after the sale, they totally sucked. Beginning in 1919, the BoSox went on a fifteen-year streak of sub-.500 seasons, losing one hundred games or more five times. Following the sale of Ruth, the Red Sox finished last in the American League nine times out of fourteen seasons.

"Frazee. The name is mud in Boston," *Boston Globe* columnist Dan Shaughnessy, author of 1990's *The Curse of the Bambino,* wrote in 2003, the year before the Sox finally broke the curse. "Come to think of it, Frazee made Boston Mudville—the place where there has been no joy at the end of every baseball season since 1918. Many New England schoolchildren can recite the sins of former Sox owner Harry Frazee. It's a tale told as often as the Midnight Ride of Paul Revere."

Harry Frazee

Even before the trade, Frazee was reviled by many. Glenn Stout wrote in "A Curse Born of Hate" for ESPN.com in 2004, that anti-Semitism whipped up by Henry Ford is its root cause. (Bostonians and many in baseball widely believed Frazee to be Jewish, even though he was actually Presbyterian.) Stout attributes the widespread notion of the "curse" and Frazee's villainy to Fred Lieb's 1947 history, *The Boston Red Sox.*

"As history, it fails entirely," Stout wrote. "As character assassination, however, it is thoroughly brilliant."

Others aren't so sure. In his 2007 book, *The Big Bam, the Life and Times of Babe Ruth,* Leigh Montville says it wasn't anti-Semitism, but Frazee who brought the infamy down on himself.

"Frazee was cast in the easily constructed role of a villain. 'The man who sold Babe Ruth,' a Boston version of Judas Iscariot," Montville wrote. "For years, long after all the characters in the drama were dead, Frazee would be seen as the despicable cur with moustache and top hat, knocking on the front door in the middle of a December night to foreclose on the widow woman and her children. Babe Ruth for *No, No, Nanette.* This was Frazee's Folly."

The question of whether misplaced anti-Semitism really played a role in the vilification of Frazee may never be answered. Clearly though, he was a man with enemies—one of whom was Byron Bancroft "Ban" Johnson, the president of the American League.

Frazee was born on June 29, 1880, in Peoria, Illinois. William Frazee and his wife Margaret could not have had any inkling that their little boy would become a famous and successful theatrical agent, producer, and director—as well as the most reviled owner of a team in the history of Boston sports. Harry died in New York on June 4, 1929, which may have been fortunate in some ways since Bostonians would probably have pinned the stock market crash later that year and the ensuing Great Depression on him, too. He has been that hated in the Hub.

Frazee had already produced a few smash hits on Broadway by the time he purchased the Red Sox in 1916. His show *Nothing But the Truth* ran for 332 performances from September 1916 to

July 1917. Frazee also owned several theater venues, including the prestigious Longacre Theatre in New York City.

Authors Michael T. Lynch Jr. (*Harry Frazee, Ban Johnson and the Feud That Nearly Destroyed the American League*) and Stout (*Red Sox Century*) argue that Frazee was actually a victim and that the sale of Ruth was the result of a long power struggle. A protracted battle pitted Frazee and two other owners, dubbed the Insurrectos, against American League president Johnson and five owners called the Loyalists. The bitter dispute came close to destroying the league Johnson had created.

Johnson disliked Frazee intensely, never approved of his purchase of the Red Sox, and wanted him out of the league. This tense situation was further exacerbated after Boston pitcher Carl Mays walked off the mound during a game in July 1919. Johnson wanted Mays suspended, but Frazee was defiant. He traded Mays to the Yankees, and the New York owners took Johnson to court when the league president tried to void the deal.

"Frazee sold Ruth for reasons beyond money that stemmed from the fact that from the moment Frazee bought the Red Sox after the 1916 season, American League president Ban Johnson tried to drive him out of the game," Stout wrote. "Johnson ran his league like a private club and Frazee hadn't asked permission to join. Over the next few years everything Frazee said and did went against the wishes of Johnson—among other things he wanted the league presidents replaced by a single commissioner—and everything Johnson did was designed to run Frazee from the game.

"Yet Johnson disliked Frazee for an even less savory reason. Just as an unwritten gentlemen's agreement kept baseball white, a similar policy prevented Jews from buying into the American League. Like many in the game Johnson looked at Frazee's New York-based theatrical background and assumed he was a Jew. Thereafter Johnson and Frazee's detractors sometimes referred to him in code, criticizing him for being too 'New York,' and referring to the 'mystery' of his religion. Few observers at the time missed the inference."

When Frazee purchased the Sox in 1916 for an estimated $500,000 from Joseph Laninin, they were loaded with great players and had won the World Series in 1912, 1915, and 1916. Laninin was the man who signed a left-handed pitcher named George Herman Ruth, a young man from Baltimore who was quite simply the best player of his day. And the Babe knew it. Ruth did what he wanted and when he wanted. Ruth was nineteen years old when he made his debut with the Sox on July 11, 1914. He beat the Cleveland Naps, 4–3.

"Legend claims that he was an orphan; the truth is his mother died when he was 16, his father when he was in the major leagues," according to Harvey Frommer of BaseballGuru.com. "His parents had placed him in St. Mary's Industrial School for Boys for his 'incorrigible' behavior: stealing, truancy, chewing tobacco and drinking whiskey. Ruth's entire youth was spent at St. Mary's where his awesome baseball talent was developed."

Ruth was a tremendous pitcher—in 1916, he beat legendary Washington Senator Walter Johnson four out of the five times they faced each other. Ruth won by scores of 5–1, 1–0, 1–0 in 13 innings, and 2–1. Ruth's nine shutouts in 1916 set an American League record for left-handers that would remain unmatched until the Yankees' Ron Guidry tied it in 1978.

The Sox, though, soon recognized that the behemoth Babe—top playing weight of 254 pounds—was even more valuable as a hitter. In 1918 the Babe only pitched twenty times but he went thirteen and seven. He also played outfield and first in seventy-two games, hit .300, and he and his teammates won the World Series again. In 1919 he pitched even less—only seventeen times—but, swinging a gargantuan forty-four-ounce bat, the Babe batted .322 with twenty-nine home runs while playing left field and first in 116 games.

Frazee cared far more about Broadway than he did about Fenway. He was often overextended on theatrical deals and constantly in need of financing. He also detested Ruth, who was loud, immature, and petulant, and threatening to sit out the 1920 season if Frazee did not double his $10,000 salary. On a cold January 5,

1920, Harry Frazee sold the twenty-four-year-old Babe to New York Yankees owner Jacob Ruppert for $125,000 and a $350,000 mortgage on Fenway.

"I should have preferred to take players in exchange for Ruth, but no club could have given me the equivalent in men without wrecking itself, and so the deal had to be made on a cash basis," Frazee told the *Boston Globe* the next day. "No other club could afford to give me the amount the Yankees have paid for him, and I don't mind saying I think they are taking a gamble. With this money the Boston club can now go into the market and buy other players and have a stronger and better team in all respects than we would have had if Ruth had remained with us."

Frazee was wrong on both counts. First of all, he did not spend the money on other players. He used it to finance a nonmusical stage play called *My Lady Friends,* which opened on Broadway in December 1919. And he kept selling off Boston's stars, mostly to the Yankees. Any gamble the New Yorkers took on Ruth paid off like a winning lottery ticket.

The Yankees would win twenty-six World Series titles—four with Ruth in the lineup—before the Sox would win another in 2004. In New York, Ruth became the most celebrated sports figure of all time, putting up staggering numbers. He revolutionized the game, changing it from a pitcher-dominated sport to one where sluggers ruled. And nobody could slug them like the Babe. In the 1924 season he won the Triple Crown with a .378 batting average, forty-six home runs, and 142 runs batted in. In 1927 he hit sixty homers, a mark that would stand for thirty-four years. The Babe was so iconic and popular that when Roger Maris hit sixty-one homers in 1961, many pointed out that the season was longer (162 games compared to 151) and demanded an asterisk in the record books next to Maris's name.

"No one hit home runs the way Babe did," his teammate Lefty Gomez once said. "They were something special. They were like homing pigeons. The ball would leave the bat, pause briefly, suddenly gain its bearings, then take off for the stands."

Frazee had a home in Boston, but his main residence—and his heart—were on Park Avenue in New York. And he was warned the Ruth deal was a poor baseball decision. When Frazee sold the slugger, Red Sox general manager Ed Barrow told him, "You ought to know that you're making a mistake."

Frazee always claimed he made the deal not because he needed the money, or because he loved the Big Apple more than Beantown. The twenty-four-year-old Ruth was already showing signs of being a diva. He was gaining weight; he had a bad knee, and was totally undisciplined. He partied to all hours even on the days when the BoSox had games, and he was not seen as a good teammate. Frazee pointed that out in the newspapers—that despite Ruth's individual heroics in 1919, the team had finished sixth. He had also skipped the final game of the season in order to play a lucrative exhibition game in Connecticut.

"It would have been impossible for us to have started the next season with Ruth and have a smooth working machine, or one that would have had any chance of being in the running," Frazee said. "Time and again Ruth has shown neither the Boston club, nor myself—nor the Boston team for that matter—much consideration. He has been rather selfish."

Despite Frazee's rationalization and Ruth's well-known penchant for partying, Boston fans were upset.

"The management of the Red Sox will have to travel some to get a player that will draw like Babe Ruth, and I am sure that the gate receipts this year will show a decided decrease now that the true sportsmanship in the game is banished and financial interests take its place," Francis J. Hurney of South Boston told the *Boston Globe* after the deal was revealed.

Longtime *Boston Globe* columnist and current ESPN panelist Bob Ryan argued in a 2001 column that Frazee deserved being "the *villain di tutti villains* in these here parts for all these years." Ryan pointed out that, instead of spending the New York money to acquire more talent, as he had promised to do, Frazee continued to sell off Boston's best players to the hated Yankees. In 1920 Barrow left the Sox and became general manager of the Yankees. Barrow knew the Red Sox players well and he spent the next few years signing all the good ones.

"The truth is that it wasn't just the sale of Ruth to the Yankees that plunged the Red Sox into the abyss (nine last-place finishes, a seventh and a sixth between 1922 and 1933)," Ryan wrote. "It was the sale of Ruth and the subsequent sales and/or trades of catcher Wally Schang, shortstop Everett Scott, and pitchers Waite Hoyt, Bullet Joe Bush, Sad Sam Jones, and Herb Pennock to the Yankees that enabled the heretofore impotent team in New York to exchange places with the team that had been a four-time world champion from 1912-18. . . . That's the crime. It wasn't just the idea that owner Harry Frazee sold Ruth to the Yankees. It's the complete package. What he did was provide New York with the complete foundation of a dynasty."

While the hated pinstripes became unquestionably the best team in baseball in the 1920s, the Sox became unquestionably the worst. In July 1923 Frazee sold the team for $1.15 million—$850,000 for the team plus the assumption of Fenway Park's $300,000 mortgage—to a group led by J. Robert Quinn and money partner Palmer Winslow.

The Sox kept losing. For years they were just plain awful and when they were actually good, they found a way to lose in heartbreaking fashion—in 1946, 1967, and 1986 the Red Sox lost the World Series in seven games. Author Stout says no one ever brought up Frazee's trading of Ruth as a curse until after the 1986 loss and then the 1990 publication of Shaughnessy's book *The Curse of the Bambino*.

"The 'Curse' fit Boston, a parochial place that always goes after the new guy, the outsider, perfectly," Stout wrote. "It made everyone an insider. Just as Boston's Brahmins once blamed the Irish for Boston's ills and the Irish blamed the Yankees and Southie blamed busing and the *Boston Globe,* the 'Curse' gave Red Sox fans someone to blame, that rat bastard Harry Frazee. He was perfect for the role: dead and a New Yorker, a patsy no one knew and who couldn't fight back. . . . The Curse was narcotic. The Curse explained everything. . . . In reality, however, the 'Curse' was just the modern manifestation of a larger, older tragedy dating back decades, and the result of a single lie that over time hijacked Red Sox history. For within the 'Curse' a faint but persistent whisper still asked, 'Wasn't Harry Frazee a Jew?'" Stout links Frazee's erroneous identification as a Jew to Henry Ford's publication of "The Jewish Degradation of American Baseball" in his weekly newspaper the *Dearborn Independent,* which was widely circulated, partially because every Ford buyer received a subscription. Frazee wasn't Jewish, but he never engaged his wrong-headed anti-Semitic detractors and once he sold the Red Sox, he left Boston and never returned.

Frazee continued to produce plays, and in 1924 he revised *My Lady Friends* into a musical and launched his biggest hit, *No, No, Nanette.* It opened in Detroit, and then reopened at the Harris Theater in Chicago and became a huge success. A year later Frazee opened the musical on Broadway to popular acclaim and it ran for 321 shows.

After *No, No, Nanette,* Frazee opened only one more Broadway production, *Yes, Yes, Yvette,* which flopped and was cancelled after forty performances. Frazee continued to live in New York and even hosted aviator Charles Lindbergh in his home, proof to baseball historians Dan and Matthew Levitt and Mark Armour that Frazee was not Jewish or the target of anti-Semitism that Stout claimed.

"Frazee organized the banquet for Lindbergh in New York City after Lindbergh's transatlantic flight in 1927, and Lindbergh stayed at Frazee's home after the flight," the three men wrote in a 2008 article in the *Baseball Research Journal.* "Although there is some debate about Lindbergh's level of anti-Semitism, it is unquestioned that he was an unrepentant eugenicist, that he made anti-Semitic speeches before the United States' entry into World War II, and that he had a close relationship with Henry Ford. After his transatlantic flight, Lindbergh could have stayed at any home in America. Would he really have chosen to stay at the home of someone perceived to be a Jew?"

Frazee died on June 4, 1929, from Bright's disease, a kidney ailment. There was no religious service and Masonic rites were performed. New York Mayor Jimmy Walker delivered the eulogy.

Seventy-five more years would pass before the Red Sox won the World Series. Frazee's progeny have long sought to clear their ancestor of wrongdoing. When the Red Sox went to the World Series in 1986 (which they famously lost in seven games), Jim Frazee wrote a defense of his great grandfather for the *Tacoma News-Tribune*. He called the Ruth sale, "the most misunderstood deal of the century."

"Despite what has often been called the worst deal in the history of baseball, Harry never lost his ambition," Jim Frazee wrote. "He made his fortune on his own skills just as Ruth was able to do . . . More often than not, Harry and Barrow had to lock Ruth in his room so he wouldn't go on all-night drinking, fighting, and womanizing sessions right up until the next game . . . I know and my family knows that Harry didn't bail on the team."

CHAPTER 14

Charles Ponzi
The Eponymous Schemer

The great abolitionist Senator Charles Sumner and legendary Speaker of the House Thomas P. "Tip" O'Neill have Boston tunnels named after them.

Beloved Boston Pops conductor Arthur Fiedler has a walkway over Storrow Drive with his name on it. The Hub's signature cable-stayed bridge over the Charles River bears the moniker of civic leader Leonard P. Zakim. The John F. Kennedy Presidential Library and Museum on Columbia Point in Dorchester honors our first Catholic president, and the good people of Beantown named the federal courthouse after Southie's great congressman Joe Moakley shortly before his death in 2001.

Only one Bostonian has a scheme named after him, though, and that would be Carlo "Charles" Ponzi.

Ponzi's name is so synonymous with screwing people out of money that people often refer to a "Ponzi Scheme" without actually knowing where the name came from. It is positively eponymous. When New York financier Bernie Madoff was sentenced to 150 years in prison in 2008 after pleading guilty to federal charges of fraud and money laundering, the news stories invariably referred to Madoff running a seven-billion-dollar "Ponzi Scheme." Just like Ponzi had victimized fellow Italian immigrants, Madoff mostly bilked fellow Jews.

You have to be some kind of incredible jerk to have a scheme named after you and Ponzi was. He could be a charming jerk with a heart of gold—he once painfully donated patches of his skin to a burn victim—but in 1919–1920, Ponzi duped between thirty thousand and forty thousand investors, mostly Italian immigrants like himself, out of at least $15 million. He promised massive returns on international postal reply coupons, which could be purchased in one country and redeemed for stamps in another. The profit was supposedly to be made on the difference in prices between countries.

Ponzi, all five-foot-two, 130 pounds of him, became a multimillionaire within a few months of starting the scheme, but newspaper reporters who had initially celebrated Ponzi in ink soon became skeptical and investigated. They learned that Ponzi was repaying investors with newer investors' money, pocketing much of it himself. He took in $20 million in a few months, equal to $222 million in current dollar values, and six banks crumbled after he was apprehended. The investigation won the *Boston Post* a Pulitzer Prize.

There were pyramid schemes before Ponzi. Just before the turn of the twentieth century, William Miller of Brooklyn, New York, cheated investors out of $1 million by claiming he had inside information on stocks. He promised his investors interest of 10 percent per week. For that, he was nicknamed "520 Percent Miller."

That scheme was nothing compared to Ponzi's, according to author Mitchell Zuckoff. Ponzi hit on the perfect combination: greed and a confident America, fresh off its World War I victory and roaring into the twenties.

"[Pyramid schemes] were called 'robbing Peter to pay Paul' before Ponzi," Zuckoff said. "We remember Ponzi because he had this amazing combination of charisma and great success, at least for a brief time. And it was this moment in 1920 where money became king and newspapers were all over it. He hit that sweet spot of money and media that elevated him and made his name indelible."

Carlo "Charles" Ponzi was born on March 3, 1882, in Lugo, a town in northern Italy, the son of postman Orestes Ponzi and his wife Imelde, whose family had fallen from the ranks of the aristocracy.

"Imelde Ponzi doted on her only child, staking her family's future on the little boy who resembled her so strongly, hoping he would restore the family to its former social and financial rank,"

Charles Ponzi with gold-handled cane and diamond stickpin

COURTESY OF THE BOSTON PUBLIC LIBRARY, LESLIE JONES COLLECTION

Zuckoff, a Boston University professor, wrote in his 2005 biography, *Ponzi's Scheme: The True Story of a Financial Legend.*

Little Carlo did restore the family fortune—for a time. When he died, he had less than $100 to his name and was buried in an unmarked pauper's grave. During his sixty-seven years on earth, he was involved in several scandals, both before and after his famous 1920 Ponzi scheme in Boston. He made and lost several fortunes and at the height of the Boston scheme lived in a 5,648-square-foot mansion in nearby Lexington, employed servants, and was driven to his office on Boston's School Street by a chauffeur in his custom-made limousine. He wore the finest clothes and strolled with a gold-handled Malacca cane in one hand and a gold-tipped cigarette holder in the other.

He had so much chutzpah that he even wrote and published an exuberant, self-celebrating autobiography after he was jailed and deported. He never apologized for stealing the nest eggs of tens of thousands. Not even close.

"Even if they never got anything for it, it was cheap at that price," he wrote of his victims in his autobiography, *The Rise of Mister Ponzi*. "Without malice aforethought I had given them the best show that was ever staged in their territory since the landing of the Pilgrims! . . . It was easily worth fifteen million bucks to watch me put the thing over!"

The twenty-one-year-old Ponzi had arrived in Boston aboard the SS *Vancouver* in 1903, following four years of intense partying at the University of Rome. He was broke and could not even speak English.

"From tie to spats, I looked like a million dollars just out of the mint, like a young gentleman of leisure," he recalled in his autobiography. "And that goes to show that appearances don't mean a thing. . . . Less than two weeks before I had left Italy with $200, a maternal blessing and a buoyant frame of mind, bound for the United States. I had sailed on a definite mission with a definite purpose; on a cinch, to get rich . . . The $200 had dwindled down to $2.50 on the way over and a card sharp had taken me for most of it, and the tips and bar the rest of it. My buoyant frame of mind was buoyant no longer."

Ponzi learned English while waiting tables, washing dishes, and doing other menial jobs in Pittsburgh, New Haven, Providence, and other East Coast cities. He had learned one lesson particularly well while at the university—he did not like to work and he aspired to be a wealthy loafer like his classmates.

"In some of the jobs I lasted no time," he wrote. "In others, I lasted longer. Often, I would be fired. Oftener, I would quit of my own accord, either disgusted or to avoid being fired. I shifted from one city to another, sometimes by rail. Sometimes by foot."

After four years of roaming, Carlo Ponzi ended up in Montreal. He changed his name to Charles Bianchi and went to work as a clerk at Banco Zarossi, which catered to the city's Italian immigrants. The bank was owned by Luigi Zarossi, who attracted customers by promising higher interest on their savings than his competitors were paying. It was a classic "robbing Peter to pay Paul" scheme because Zarossi was actually dipping into the funds young Italian workers were sending home to their families. It worked, for a while, and business boomed. Ponzi/Bianchi was promoted to bank manager and, always a flirt, he began dating Zarossi's seventeen-year-old daughter, Angelina.

The end came quickly for Banco Zarossi. When customers started complaining that the earnings they were sending home never arrived, Luigi Zarossi filled a suitcase full of money and fled to Mexico. Another employee disappeared and one killed himself. The bank failed. Ponzi stayed, and even cared for Angelina, her three sisters, and her mother for a few months. He then decided to leave and forged a check from another bank for $423.58. Always sartorially conscious, he spent half of that on new clothing and was arrested. "Charles Ponzi, alias Bianchi" was sentenced to three years in jail. He was paroled after twenty months but was arrested again, this time by US officials who nabbed him at the border and accused him of aiding five other Italians who were trying to illegally enter the United States. He served another two years in a federal prison in Atlanta.

When he left that prison, he started drifting again and ended up in a coal-mining town, Blocton, Alabama, where he translated for the Italian miners and their families and attempted to organize the miners into a community, which he expected to head and for which he also anticipated he would be paid handsomely. That didn't work out, but while there, a nurse named Pearl Gossett was badly burned in a cooking accident, and Ponzi volunteered large swaths of his skin for her grafts. Even swindlers have a nice side.

In 1917 he headed back to Boston. He met petite Rose Gnecco on a streetcar and began wooing her. She was taken with her older, sophisticated suitor and they married in February 1918. Ponzi took over her father's grocery business and proceeded to ruin it. Then the idea that would make Ponzi rich, famous, and, eventually, infamous, literally fell into his hands.

Ponzi had just opened a letter from Spain when a little international postal reply coupon, enclosed for reply postage, fell out. It had been purchased in Spain for thirty centavos and it could be exchanged for a US postage stamp worth five cents, the rate set by international treaty. Ponzi knew that the Spanish peso was down in relation to the dollar and figured that someone who bought a postal reply coupon in Spain could redeem it in the United States for a 10 percent profit. Ponzi then decided that purchasing coupons in countries with weaker economies could increase that margin even more. He thought he could make a killing by making large-scale purchases of postal reply coupons. He founded the Securities Exchange Company and started promoting his idea, claiming to potential investors that he had a network of hundreds of agents around the world.

"It was a big idea—one that Ponzi managed to sell to thousands of people," Mary Darby wrote in *Smithsonian* magazine in 1998. "Of course, there was no network of agents. . . . A final audit of his company's assets after the whole business was over turned up $61 worth of the coupons."

In other words, Ponzi was scheming from the start to separate his investors—mostly working-class Italians in Boston—from their hard-earned cash. He showed up at bocce games and bistros promising a 150 percent return in ninety days. He later shortened it to forty-five days.

The money began to roll in.

"Once Ponzi paid off his first round of investors, word of the financial 'wizard' on School Street spread quickly," Darby wrote. "Ultimately, some 40,000 people joined the feeding frenzy. Many people simply reinvested their profits with Ponzi, thereby relieving him of actually having to make good on his promise. At the height of his success, Ponzi had offices from Maine to New Jersey."

Newspapers in July 1920 became aware of Ponzi when a furniture salesman named Joseph Daniels filed a $1 million suit against Ponzi for an old debt. By then, Ponzi had bought his mansion in Lexington, his custom-made limo, diamonds and pearls for Rose, gold-tipped cigarette holders and Malacca canes for himself, commercial and rental properties all over Boston, and bank stocks. He even arranged a takeover of the Hanover Trust.

Newspaper coverage was fawning at first. On July 24, a two-column headline on the *Boston Post's* front page screamed "Doubles the Money Within Three Months," with a subhead "50 Per Cent Interest Paid in 45 Days by Ponzi—Has Thousands of Investors." In the story, the thirty-eight-year-old Ponzi told the reporter he was worth $8.5 million. "Always I have said to myself, if I can get one million dollars I can live with all the comfort I want for the rest of my life. If I get one million dollars, I will spend all over and above the one million trying to do good in the world. Now I have that million."

On Monday, July 26, investors lined up four abreast along City Hall Avenue and School Street.

"Hope and greed could be read in everybody's countenance . . . wads of money nervously clutched and waved by thousands of outstretched fists," Ponzi wrote later. "Madness, money madness, the worst kind of madness, was reflected in everybody's eyes! . . . To the crowd there assembled, I was the realization of their dreams. . . . The 'wizard' who could turn a pauper into a millionaire overnight!"

Federal, state, and postal authorities had been investigating Ponzi since February 1920 but had made little progress. *Boston Post* publisher Richard Grozier also became dubious, and launched his own investigation. Soon the *Post* stories were quoting financial experts saying there was no way Ponzi could be legitimate. Even 520 Percent Miller, now reformed after a stretch in Sing Sing and known as "Honest Miller," was quoted as saying Ponzi was a fraud. One reporter discovered that only eight dollars' worth of postal reply coupons had been redeemed per day over the last few months.

"Why don't the postal operations reflect Ponzi's, if he is truly dealing in millions of coupons?" the *Post* story asked. "And why does he keep such large amounts of money—several million in Boston banks and $5 million abroad, he claims—in institutions and holdings that only pay him 5% while he claims to send the investors' fund overseas to earn 400%?"

Frightened investors began demanding their money back. On one day alone, Ponzi refunded more than a million dollars. Always the dapper showman, Ponzi ordered coffee and sandwiches for the anxious throngs outside his office and asked that women be allowed to claim their refunds first so they wouldn't faint while waiting in the July heat. The feds closed in and the final straw came when Ponzi's publicity director, a former newspaperman named William McMasters, turned Judas.

On August 2, the *Post* ran a copyrighted, first-person report penned by McMasters in which he proclaimed Ponzi hopelessly insolvent. "He is over $2,000,000 in debt even if he tried to meet his notes without paying any interest," McMasters wrote. "If the interest is included on his outstanding notes, then he is at least $4,500,000 in debt."

Ponzi managed to keep his charade going for nine more days, but on August 11, the *Post* revealed that Ponzi had done time in Canada for forging checks. The next day a federal government auditor concluded his examination of Ponzi's books. He found Ponzi to be $3 million in debt (later revised to $7 million). Ponzi was arrested and jailed in East Cambridge.

Six banks crashed in the aftermath of Ponzi's fall. His investors lost 70 cents on each dollar they gave Ponzi. The *Boston Post* won journalism's top award for its reporting on the scheme.

Ponzi was convicted on eighty-two federal counts of using the mail to defraud. He served three and a half years before he was paroled. In 1925 he was convicted on state fraud charges. While that verdict was under appeal, he headed for Florida on bail and, using the name Charpon, began selling swampland for development. He was arrested in Florida and charged with fraud there. He jumped bail when he learned his conviction in Massachusetts had been upheld. Now wanted in two states, Ponzi fled to Texas. He got a job as a crew member on an Italian freighter, but was apprehended when the ship docked in New Orleans. Ponzi was returned to Massachusetts and locked up in the state prison in Charlestown for seven and a half years.

After Ponzi was released in 1934, he was deported to Italy as an undesirable alien. Rose told reporters, "Charles is a victim of circumstance" and waited patiently for two more years for Ponzi to send for her. He didn't, and she finally divorced him in 1936. For the rest of her life, according to Donald Dunn, author of *Ponzi! The Boston Swindler,* she was dogged by rumors that she had secretly squirreled away her ex-husband's profits. She eventually remarried and moved to Florida and told Dunn in an interview shortly before she died that not only did Ponzi leave her penniless; he had actually defrauded her and eight of her relatives out of $16,000 they had loaned him.

Ponzi ended up in Brazil, where he taught English and French and worked as an interpreter for an Italian importing firm. His eyesight began failing and he suffered a paralyzing stroke in 1948. Rose did not answer the many letters he wrote to her. He died alone in a charity hospital in Rio de Janeiro on January 18, 1949, leaving just $75 in a bank account and a copy of his autobiography on the table next to his bed.

CHAPTER 15

Barney Welansky
"I only wish I had been at the fire and died with the others"

On November 26, 1946, a feeble and emaciated man walked out of the state prison in Norfolk, Massachusetts. Barnett "Barney" Welansky was only forty-nine years old, but he looked much older. He was terminally sick with lung and throat cancer, and with bitterness.

"I only wish," he told reporters, "I had been at the fire and died with the others."

The fire, four years earlier at Welansky's swanky Cocoanut Grove nightclub on Piedmont Street in Park Square, claimed 492 lives. Welansky was the only person who served any time in prison, although Bostonians believed then, and many believe still, that plenty of other people—including the man who pardoned him— deserved at least some of the blame.

"If you were wrongfully convicted—framed—you'd feel you had a perfect right to be free," the embittered Welansky told the reporters.

To be clear, Welansky was not framed. As owner of Boston's most popular nightclub, he had cut corners, completed unlicensed renovations on the cheap, ignored building codes and capacity codes, illegally stockpiled untaxed liquor, and paid off politicians and inspectors with free drinks and meals. He also locked doors and blocked off exits so no one could beat a check, creating the scenario that would burst into a fiery living hell on November 28, 1942.

Other hands were dirty too: The fire department inspector who had reported a "sufficient number of exits" and "no inflammable decorations" just days before the fire. The police captain who was drinking with Welansky's brother Jimmy in the Grove that Saturday evening, conveniently ignoring that the nightclub was packed to more than twice its licensed capacity. The mayor, Maurice J. Tobin, who Welansky had bragged about being "in" with, and who after the fire reportedly attended the wake of nineteen-year-old Mary McCormack, daughter of Edward "Knocko" McCormack, a Southie politico.

"The mayor . . . attempted to express his condolences to Knocko, who would have none of it," John Esposito wrote in *Fire in the Grove*. "The grieving father believed that the mayor bore some responsibility for his daughter's death. According to the story, Knocko brushed aside Tobin's outstretched hand and punched the mayor in the face."

The Cocoanut Grove fire—the worst nightclub fire in US history—left a scar on Boston that has never completely healed. Years later, revelers who escaped and firefighters who responded remembered terrible details—the smell of burning flesh; patrons' hair bursting into flames; the pretty young woman untouched by the blaze found by a firefighter still sitting at her table with a drink in her hand, dead, her lungs melted; the eight-high piles of bodies at the jammed revolving door and at the locked exit doors; and the ball of superheated toxic flames that raced from room to room in the overcrowded club.

"So many bodies were being pulled out of the club that rescue workers were forced to make terrible decisions, trying to determine those who were still alive and getting them to transport, and piling the corpses like cordwood on the sidewalk," Stephanie Schorow wrote in *The Cocoanut Grove Fire*.

The horrors of the blaze, just one year after Pearl Harbor, briefly knocked World War II off the front pages of the nation's newspapers. Cocoanut Grove changed the way buildings are inspected and the way burn victims are treated. Ten people were indicted and many more could have been—a boxful of chits for free meals that were signed by "names you won't have to ask us how to spell" as one detective told reporters—and other Cocoanut Grove records mysteriously disappeared. Welansky was the only one who went to prison, but Bostonians felt the malfeasance went

far beyond Barney cutting corners, or busboy Stanley Tomaszewski accidentally setting a fake palm tree in the basement Melody
Lounge on fire.

"The blame should not be on the shoulders of this 16-year-old
boy," one furious letter writer wrote to the *Boston Globe* a few days
after the fire, "but rather on the heads of all the corrupt officials
whose hands were greased with money."

For his part, Barney, whose entire decadelong involvement
with the club smacked of shadiness, somehow remained convinced
that he had been screwed. A lawyer, he had been disbarred while
in jail and, with his brother, convicted of federal tax evasion. The
surviving victims and the relatives of the 492 dead received just
$150 each after the Grove's assets—mostly Barney's hidden cache
of untaxed liquor—were sold off. Welansky didn't even carry liability insurance and his fire insurance topped out at $20,000.

Still, "I was the victim," Welansky reportedly told an attorney who visited him in jail. "I took the blame for the power and
authorities at the time."

Barney Welansky was born in Boston in 1896, one of six kids
of poor Russian-Jewish immigrants. He grew up in Boston's tough
West End and sold newspapers on the corner to earn money.
The chubby teen did so well that the news dealers assigned him
a prime spot at Boylston Street and Massachusetts Avenue. By
the time he was twenty-one, he had earned his bachelor's and law
degrees from Boston University, and in 1919 he became a partner
of well-regarded Attorney Herbert F. Callahan.

"Barney Welansky's personal journey had been in so many
ways the classic American story of the child of immigrants who
had steadily climbed the ladder of success through personal discipline, hard work, and education," Esposito wrote.

Entertainers Mickey Albert and Jacques Renard originally
opened Cocoanut Grove in 1927 during Prohibition as a supper
club—soft drinks only but setups available for those with their
own bottles. The club, on narrow Piedmont Street just off the theater district, foundered after the stock market crashed in 1929,

and the musicians grabbed the $10,000 offered them for the club by gangster Charles "King" Solomon in 1931 through his attorney, Barney Welansky. Solomon, a heroin smuggler and loan shark, ran Cocoanut Grove like a personal playground—bringing in Guy Lombardo, Jimmy Durante, and other big names he couldn't afford during the Depression—and he lost a lot of his ill-gotten dough in the club.

"His darkest legacy—a tradition that doomed patrons a decade later—rose from his darkest fears: he made sure exit doors to the club were locked inside and out," Schorow wrote. "No one could sneak up on him and no one—neither patron nor employee—could run out on a bill."

Welansky became the attorney for King Solomon's estate in January 1933 when the justifiably paranoid Solomon was shot dead in the men's room of the Cotton Club in Roxbury. Welansky "inherited" Cocoanut Grove because its value was listed as zero and "the estate didn't want it," he later claimed. To be fair, Cocoanut Grove was hemorrhaging cash while King Solomon owned it.

"By the time Barney took over, the place was a money pit," Esposito wrote.

Welansky got a huge break when Congress repealed Prohibition in December 1933. People were drinking again—legally anyway—and Barney began building his empire. (He rehired Mickey Alpert as musical director and hired Rose Gnecco, the former Rose Ponzi, divorced wife of the eponymous swindler, as his bookkeeper.)

In Cocoanut Grove, Barney had found the love of his life. He immediately began adding onto the original 3,200-square-foot club, and by the time of the fire he had constructed Boston's most elegant and elaborate nightclub—with four bars in three rooms—two at street level and, one, the Melody Lounge, in the basement. The upstairs roof could be rolled back in fair weather for dancing under the stars.

Within nine years after Welansky "inherited" Cocoanut Grove, he stopped practicing law and spent all his time running his pride and joy. He and his wife had no kids and Barney never showed any interest in the showgirls or beautiful women who hung out at the Cocoanut Grove. He was pudgy and wore rumpled suits and worked relentlessly at the Grove, always cutting corners and doing anything legal or illegal to make more money. He loved having politicians and bigwigs beholden to him—he signed off on their checks and then kept every one of them. One consultant later testified that Welansky bragged to him the month before the fire that it didn't matter that the electrician he hired to wire the Grove's new room, the New Broadway Lounge, was unlicensed. "I fit with Tobin," Welansky allegedly told the man. "They owe me plenty."

Just forty-five, Barney suffered a heart attack twelve days before the fire and was hospitalized in Massachusetts General. His younger brother Jimmy, a tougher customer who had been arrested for the murder of a mobster in 1937 but never indicted, watched over the club while Barney was in the hospital. He reported to Barney that business was booming, and at about 10 p.m. on Saturday, November 28, 1942—despite the Boston College football team canceling its victory party after being upset by Holy Cross—the place was packed. Jimmy Welansky sat in the New Broadway Lounge, opened the previous day on a fraudulently obtained license, enjoying a drink or three with a Suffolk County assistant district attorney and Boston Police Captain Joseph A. Buccigross. The captain, in plain clothes and ostensibly there on an inspection, conveniently failed to notice the Grove was at more than double its capacity of 460. Married couples, soldiers and sailors on leave, wedding parties, players and wannabes, movie star Buck Jones—it seemed everyone wanted to be in the Grove that night.

Waiters positioned extra tables everywhere there was a bare patch of floor—aisles, corridors, walkways, in front of locked exits and barred windows. Downstairs in the Melody Lounge, a piano player banged out "Bell Bottom Trousers." A soldier and his girl, wanting privacy, unscrewed a low-wattage bulb in a fake palm tree. Stanley Tomaszewski, the sixteen-year-old busboy, told by bartender John Bradley to restore the light, climbed onto a chair

The Cocoanut Grove Lounge after the horrific fire that claimed nearly 500 lives
COURTESY OF THE BOSTON FIRE HISTORICAL SOCIETY

and struck a match to find the socket hidden in the fronds. As he turned away, someone shouted the tree was on fire. Stanley and Bradley and other Grove employees tried to throw water on the flames and pull down the tree, "like Keystone Kops in white shirts and aprons," Esposito wrote, amusing some in the packed room. They got the tree down in less than a minute, but suddenly, fire swept across the fabric ceiling. The entire ceiling of the Melody Lounge burst into blue and orange flames and then the flames were sucked like a well-drafted fire up the chimney-like stairs. Panic ensued. Some patrons' hair burst into flames, and men and women screamed in the smoke-filled, windowless darkness. Tomaszewski led a few patrons through the kitchen to find an exit, but hundreds of other customers headed for the flame-filled stairs, the only exit they could see. Many never got there—a few people caught on fire, many suffocated on the smoke, others literally had their lungs fried by a blast of 1,800-degree air and dropped dead as they stood up. The first people to reach the stairs were clawed at and pulled back by others. Some caught on fire. Bodies began to pile up in the stairs. Husbands were separated from their wives, friends from friends, lovers from lovers, never to see one another again.

The fire had only been burning two or three minutes at that point. The toxic flames would soon burst into the main floor where seven hundred or more patrons were blissfully ignorant of what awaited.

The fireball roared up the four-foot-wide stairs and into the Grove's foyer and dining room, where Alpert was just about to take the stage for his second set of the night. Hundreds of patrons immediately panicked.

"With their hair on fire and their skin blistering, people scrambled for the only exit they knew—the revolving door, which was jammed, with bodies rapidly piling up behind it," Schorow wrote. Patrons and employees managed to force open a locked door to Shawmut Street and poured out. "Unfortunately, fire also seeks air. As oxygen in the dining room was depleted, the flames roared toward the Shawmut Street door, turning the precious opening into a roaring blaze, trapping those inside who had not yet escaped."

Within just a few minutes, hundreds of those people would be dead, killed in the worst nightclub fire in US history and the second worst of any building fire, other than the terrorists' attacks on the twin towers in New York City on September 11, 2001. The worst single building fire was the Iroquois Theatre fire in Chicago on December 30, 1903, which claimed 603 lives, most of them children.

The first alarm for the Cocoanut Grove fire was rung in just fifteen minutes after the fire started—but it was actually rung for a car fire at the nearby corner of Stuart and Carver Streets. Engine Company 22's firefighters took less than a minute to put out the car fire, but then one noticed thick black smoke pouring into the night sky from just a few blocks away. The firefighters rushed to the Grove and a scene of horror so unimaginable that many of the firefighters, as well as many of the patrons, could not talk about it for years. The revolving doors to the main foyer were already jammed, with bodies piling up behind them. Flames were pouring out of the door of the New Broadway Lounge and also out of the Shawmut Street door, where firefighter Charles Kenney of Rescue One ran.

"Kenney saw, in a pile of bodies, a woman's small hand desperately waving," Schorow wrote. "'Hold on, Sister, Hold on,' he cried and firmly grabbed her wrist, even though he could feel his fingers sinking down through burned flesh to the bone. . . . He could feel her hand grabbing his, grabbing with all her strength. He managed to pull the woman to her feet. Her clothes were torn away but Dotty Myles was carried out alive. Kenney continued his rescue work until he collapsed and was taken to a hospital. Doctors later found claw marks on his legs, evidence of the frantic appeals of dying club patrons."

Within minutes, the narrow streets and alleys around the club became a macabre nightmare with screaming and injured patrons looking in the piles of dead for their spouses and friends. At the main entrance, flames leaped out twenty feet. The heat from the fire was so intense, the revolving door so jammed, that initially all the firefighters could do was train their hoses on the entrance and watch helplessly as the people behind the glass burned to death.

The dead and dying were stacked up on the sidewalks. Taxi cabs, private vehicles, police cars, anything with wheels, were pressed into ambulance service as victims were rushed to Boston City, Mass General and other area hospitals. The seventeen-year-old singer that Kenney had rescued was one of them.

"Dotty Myles sat dazed on the sidewalk, apparently no one thought she would live," Schorow wrote. "Gathering her strength, she leaped into an ambulance already packed with victims. When it reached Boston City Hospital, she was the only one alive."

Seventy-five of the one hundred and fourteen victims transported to Massachusetts General, where Barney Welansky lay recovering from his heart attack, were dead on arrival or died before the night was over. Three hundred victims were taken to Boston City Hospital—one hundred and sixty-eight were DOA, thirty-six more died shortly after arrival.

Seven of the thirty-nine victims who survived the night at Mass General subsequently died, all of respiratory complications and none from burns. (An eighth Mass General patient, whose wife had died, lived despite his injuries but later leaped through a closed window to his death because of his survivor's guilt.) At Boston City, thirty-nine of the ninety-six Cocoanut Grove patients who survived the first night later died from a combination of burns and respiratory complications. The techniques developed for burn victims at Mass General by Dr. Oliver Cope soon changed the way burns would be treated around the world.

The most famous burn survivor, however, was treated at Boston City Hospital by Dr. Newton Browder. Coast Guardsman Clifford Johnson had raced back into the Grove several times, failing to find his date but able to rescue other people. "He emerged from the last attempt a ball of flames and fell on the sidewalk," Esposito wrote. Johnson, a strapping farm boy from Missouri, endured more than thirty thousand pinprick skin grafts over the next twenty-one months. He married one of his nurses and moved to his hometown, where he became a game warden. In 1956 Johnson's car skidded off the road and he was burned to death when it burst into flames.

Within days of the Cocoanut Grove disaster, state Attorney General Robert Bushnell announced that his investigation to affix blame would "dig down to the last grain of sand and no one will be spared . . . whether he be an official or private citizen." Fire Commissioner William Reilly also held hearings over the next two months to find the cause of the fire. He determined it was impossible to say with certainty that the busboy's match, and not an electrical malfunction or something else, was the cause and "unknown origin" was entered into his report.

"Perhaps the most important part of the report was the section on recommendations, because many of them were enacted into law, not just in Boston and Massachusetts, but throughout the country," Jerome M. Chertkoff and Russell H. Kushigian wrote in *Don't Panic: The Psychology of Emergency Egress and Ingress*. "There should be automatic sprinklers in every room. If a basement is a place of assembly, there should be at least two direct means of access to the street, and a metal-covered automatic-closing fire door between the basement and the first floor. Exit doors should have panic locks and no others. Exits should be marked by 'EXIT' signs, powered by a supplementary electrical system unaffected by a failure of the main system."

The grand jury indicted ten people, including Barney Welansky, for manslaughter, and James Welansky for accessory after the fact of manslaughter and willful neglect of duty. Wine steward Jacob Goldfine, who allegedly blocked an exit shouting, "Nobody goes out until he pays his check," was also indicted for manslaughter. Fire Lieutenant Frank Linney, the inspector who reported a sufficient number of exits days before the blaze, was indicted for willful and corrupt neglect of duty. Joseph Buccigross, the police captain who was drinking with Jimmy Welansky when the fire broke out, was indicted for conspiracy to violate building laws. The club's architect, the building commissioner, a building inspector, and Samuel Rudnick, who was the builder of the New Broadway Lounge, along with Rudnick's building foreman, were also indicted. It was rumored, Esposito wrote, that the twenty-two grand jurors almost indicted Mayor Tobin but fell short by a single vote.

Besides Barney Welansky, Rudnick was the only defendant found guilty, and his prison sentence was suspended. Barney was tried as a codefendant with his brother and Goldfine in the manslaughter of nineteen of the 492 victims. Prosecutors chose the representative nineteen victims in two ways. Some were chosen because of the way they died and their locations—burned to death at the revolving door, for example, or suffocated in front of a door bolted shut. Others were chosen for emotional impact, such as the couple who decided to have "one last dance" before the ballroom burst into flames.

Herbert Callahan, representing his old partner, told the jury "no man could have reasonably anticipated what happened at Cocoanut Grove on the night of November 28." He argued the loss of life was caused by panic. Assistant District Attorney Frederick T. Doyle ripped into the defendants. He said they, especially Barney, were motivated to keep the exits locked by greed and called the panic defense "a libel on the dead."

The jury was out four hours and fifty minutes. Goldfine and Jimmy Welansky both cried when they heard the foreman read "not guilty" after their names nineteen times. Barney showed no emotion as he heard his name and "guilty" an equal number. At Barney's sentencing the next week, Attorney General Bushnell acknowledged, "Barnett Welansky could not alone have created these conditions" and invited Barney to name names "instead of blaming the dead." Bushnell added, "We would like to know things only Mr. Welansky knows."

The judge sentenced Barney Welansky to twelve to fifteen years in state prison. Barney never named names. He served almost four years before he was diagnosed with terminal throat and lung cancer. In November 1946 his old pal and mayoral drinking buddy, Maurice Tobin, by then governor, pardoned him.

Barney Welansky, bitter and broken, died five months later.

CHAPTER 16

Specs O'Keefe
"Songbird" of the Brink's Gang

Just after 7 p.m. on January 17, 1950, seven armed men wearing Halloween masks, chauffeur's caps, gloves, Navy-style peacoats, and rubber overshoes robbed the Brink's Incorporated counting house in the North End of $1.2 million in cash and another $1.6 million in checks and securities. At the time, it was the biggest cash haul ever in a robbery in the United States. No one was hurt and no shots were fired.

Bostonians were shocked the next day to learn about what the *Boston Daily Globe, Boston Post, Daily Record, Boston Evening American, Boston Traveler,* and *Boston Herald* all described as the "perfect crime" and "crime of the century." When Brink's president John D. Allen arrived from his headquarters in Chicago and offered a $100,000 reward for the robbers, dead or alive, and then added, "We'd rather have them dead," the Hub's citizens had already begun to think of the robbers as local heroes.

"The temptation is almost to congratulate the thieves upon winning the world championship, and that, of course, is terribly, terribly wrong," *Boston Herald* columnist Bill Cunningham wrote three days after the holdup. "For some, crossed-up reason, however, the ringing pronouncement of the spokesman of the victimized agency that he'll pay $100,000 for the Halloweenized drill squad alive or dead, and 'preferably dead,' fails to inspire a ringing Amen. . . . [The robbery] was so stupendous, so completely and expertly done, that it's hard to remember we're on the side of the stupid company and the confounded police force. Our teammates in that one look so silly, the impulse is to disown 'em."

One Bostonian tried to disown the robbers instead. Mayor John B. Hynes told the *Herald* the holdup "was the work of a well-organized gang of out-of-town criminals whose habits are unknown to our police." But as the crime became more celebrated—and as it became obvious local wise guys had pulled off the heist—most Bostonians embraced it. Comedians everywhere were making Brink's the punch line of their jokes. On the immensely popular *Ed Sullivan Show,* the host trotted out a group of men wearing masks and introduced them as the Brink's robbers to a huge laugh from the studio and home audience. Over the next six years— until just days before the state statute of limitations would have expired—the Brink's robbers avoided arrests and became Bean-town folk heroes.

"The good citizens of Boston . . . applauded the daring nature of the crime," wrote Stephanie Schorow in her 2008 book, *The Crime of the Century: How the Brink's Robbers Stole Millions and the Hearts of Boston.* "They chuckled over the ease with which a counting house of the fabled Brink's armored car service was raided by men in Halloween masks who never fired a shot. And 'no one got hurt' was the oft-repeated coda. For six years the robbers outwitted, outfoxed, and outlasted the best efforts of the FBI and Boston Police. And, old-time Bostonians will solemnly add, if one of the robbers hadn't decided to rat out his fellow thieves, they would have gotten away with it."

That rat was Specs O'Keefe.

Joseph James O'Keefe was born in South Boston on March 30, 1908, the seventh of Edward Cornelius and Catherine (Hurney) O'Keefe's sixteen children. Like many of the Irish in Boston at the time, the O'Keefes were dirt poor. Edward worked at the city's jail on Deer Island in Boston Harbor. The family lived in a six-room apartment without running water. Specs got his nick-name, not from wearing glasses or his freckles, but from begging for bananas from a street vendor in Southie. The vendor would give him overripe bananas already showing brown speckles, and thus Joseph James became Specky, a moniker often later short-ened to Specs.

He was in and out of trouble all of his life.

Specky was caught stealing from a candy store when he was eight and stole a horse and wagon when he was nine. After several more arrests he was sent to the Lyman School reformatory in Westboro where the staff reported his home life "lacked restraint." Back in Boston, his crimes steadily became more serious, and in December 1927 he was sentenced to five years in the state prison in Concord after a breaking-and-entering conviction.

The slender and always well-dressed O'Keefe was "well informed, exhibited a wry sense of humor, had a keen memory for details, and despite years in jail, was sharp—a fascinating mixture of contradictory human qualities," FBI special agent in charge Edwin Powers years later told the *Boston Globe*. Specs was also a cool customer and handy with a gun.

In 1932 after yet another conviction, he was sent to the Deer Island House of Correction where his father had once worked. He and another inmate escaped a few days before Christmas. When their rowboat filled with water before they could even get into it, they decided to swim to freedom and plunged into the icy waters of Boston Harbor. They made it to shore in nearby Winthrop. Specky took off to New York City where he continued his criminal ways. Then he met pretty Mary Gerst, an Ohio girl, married, and decided to go straight. They moved to Defiance, Ohio, where Specky worked low-paying jobs until he returned to Massachusetts to roll a few bookies and help out in a shoe factory payroll robbery being planned by a friend, Michael "Vinnie" Geagan. He made $1,250 on the payroll job and returned to Ohio, but shortly after that was arrested as a fugitive and extradited to Massachusetts to complete his old sentence.

Mary came to Massachusetts, too, and when Specky was released they adopted a boy, David, from a woman Specky met in a bar. Specky insisted he loved Mary even though he always had a girl on the side.

"I was never good enough for Mary and I never will be," O'Keefe said in a 1961 as-told-to book, *The Men who Robbed Brink's,* authored with Bob Considine. "Mary was always a very decent, a very clean girl, too wonderful for me."

Joseph "Specs" O'Keefe

COURTESY OF THE BOSTON PUBLIC LIBRARY, LESLIE JONES COLLECTION

Once released, Specs hooked up with Tony Pino, Vincent Costa, Vinnie Geagan, Adolph "Jazz" Maffie, Joseph McGinnis, Sandy Richardson, James "Jimma" Flaherty, and Stanley "Gus" Gusciora, all career criminals. They became a formidable gang.

"Daring and brazenness were considered achievements," Schorow wrote, "but so was the ability to do time and keep your mouth shut. By the late 1940s, Pino's crew was well up in the hierarchy of the rackets; the men were middle-aged with families to support, and looking far older than their years from the effects of too much booze, cigarettes and stress."

On October 30, 1947, Pino and some of the gang, but not O'Keefe, robbed the B. F. Sturtevant Company in Hyde Park of its $110,000 payroll. The next day they held up the American Sugar Refining Company in South Boston for its payroll of $29,000. Only one gang member was ever convicted in the Sturtevant robbery, none in the American Sugar job. Both payrolls had been delivered by Brink's.

Pino soon began planning the Great Brink's Robbery. "Pino was known in the underworld as an excellent 'case man,'" according to an FBI narrative. "And it was said that the 'casing' of the Brink's offices bore his 'trademark.'"

Born in Sicily in 1907, Tony "The Pig" Pino was just eight months old when he entered the United States, but he never became a naturalized citizen. Like O'Keefe, Pino had entered early into a life of crime while growing up in Southie. At fifteen, he was shot in the buttocks while trying to run from the cops. At twenty-one, he did a year and a half in Concord Reformatory for "carnal abuse" of a fifteen-year-old girl. It was during that stint that he became reacquainted and friends with Specs and the other cons that would later join him on the Brink's job.

In November 1937, Pino and four other men were discovered trying to crack a safe in the basement of a Back Bay store. A free-for-all with police ensued and some of the robbers were knocked unconscious. Pino was sentenced to consecutive three- to four-year terms in Charlestown State Prison.

Still, "Pino's obsession with Brink's was uncontrollable," according to Schorow. "He was going to take the company in a way no one had ever dreamed of." He began to assemble his team of safecrackers, getaway car drivers, and guys like Specky and Gusciora who could handle a gun.

"Although basically the 'brain child' of Pino, the Brink's robbery was the product of the combined thought and criminal experience of men who had known each other for many years," according to the FBI's narrative. "Serious consideration originally had been given to robbing Brink's in 1947, when Brink's was located on Federal Street in Boston. . . .Their plan was to enter the Brink's building and take a truck containing payrolls. Many problems and dangers were involved in such a robbery, and the plans never crystallized."

Pino remained fixated on Brink's, though, and soon settled on Brink's North Terminal Garage on Prince Street. The planning took years, and included watching the Brink's operation from a nearby roof with a telescope.

"Police detectives called them brilliant, cunning," the *Boston Globe's* Cindy Rodriguez wrote in 1999. "It turned out they were 11 middle-aged males with time on their hands. The men, most of them petty thieves, spent two years planning what came to be known as The Great Brink's Robbery. They studied the layout of the armored-car garage on Prince and Commercial streets. Several times, they walked inside in stocking feet. They measured distances, eyed escape routes. One night, the men removed the locks from several doors, fitted keys to them, and replaced them. A month before the robbery, they ran through a dress rehearsal. And all that time, even with patrolling guards, no one suspected."

The gang was appalled at the inadequacy of the Brink's security. According to Noel Behn, author of *Big Stick-Up at Brink's!,* Specs brought one of his girlfriends along for a tour on one of the nights the robbers cased the garage.

On raw and cold January 17, 1950, the real deal went down. The Celtics were playing the Minneapolis Lakers nearby at the Garden. Buxom actress Jane Russell was appearing on stage at the RKO-Boston Theater on Washington Street. A poultry show was clucking along at the old Mechanics Building on Huntington Avenue. Just after 7 p.m., seven men stealthily crept into the Brink's North Terminal Garage. Clutching long-barrel revolvers, they opened three cage doors and stepped into the vault. They pointed their guns at the five Brink's employees who had been counting money, ordered them to lie on the floor, tied them up and taped their mouths shut.

"The robbers did little talking," according to the FBI narrative. "They moved with a studied precision which suggested that the crime had been carefully planned and rehearsed in the preceding months."

Within minutes, the robbers were filling canvas bags with cash and dragging them out the door to a 1949 Ford stake-body truck stolen from a Ford dealership in November. By the time one of the Brink's clerks got his hands untied and called the police, the seven robbers and their four lookouts were long gone and, as it would turn out, very hard to find.

"It never dawned on anyone that someone would attempt that kind of robbery," Barry Mawn, special agent in charge of the FBI office in Boston, told the *Globe* in a 1999 interview. "Nothing of that nature had ever been attempted."

Pino's planning and the gang's execution had been flawless. The Boston Police were embarrassed. In the coming months and years, J. Edgar Hoover would assign four hundred FBI agents to the case.

The Boston Police immediately began picking up and questioning well-known Boston hoods. Veteran criminals throughout the United States also felt the heat, and racetracks and casinos were instructed to be on the lookout for certain bills—some of the loot was marked—or for gamblers with unusually large sums of cash.

"A systematic check of current and past Brink's employees was undertaken," according to the FBI. "Personnel of the three-story building housing the Brink's offices were questioned; inquiries were made concerning salesmen, messengers, and others who had called at Brink's and might know its physical layout as well as its operational procedures. . . . All identifying marks placed on currency and securities by the customers were noted, and appropriate 'stops' were placed at banking institutions across the Nation."

The FBI and Boston Police were flooded with tips and theories on who the criminals were, ranging from communists intent on overthrowing the government to suddenly flush ex-husbands.

The eleven members of the Brink's gang—Specs O'Keefe, Jazz Maffie, Anthony Pino, Thomas Richardson, Joseph McGinnis, Stanley Gusciora, Vincent Costa, Joseph Banfield, Henry Baker, Vinnie Geagan, and Jimma Flaherty—were among the strong early suspects. They all had alibis, albeit shaky ones, and law officials could find no evidence to arrest them. The gang members all laid low; they had agreed to spend their ill-gotten cash in small sums only. Specs pocketed $5,000 and gave the rest of his share to Jazz to hold.

On June 2, O'Keefe and Gusciora left town, allegedly to visit Gus's dead brother's grave in Missouri. They were arrested in Towanda, Pennsylvania, for burglaries in two western Pennsylvania communities. On September 8, O'Keefe was sentenced to three years in the Bradford County Jail. On October 11, Gusciora was sentenced to serve from five to twenty years in the Western Pennsylvania Penitentiary.

"Even after these convictions, O'Keefe and Gusciora continued to seek their release," according to the FBI narrative. "Between 1950 and 1954, the underworld occasionally rumbled with rumors that pressure was being exerted upon Boston hoodlums to contribute money for these criminals' legal fight against the charges in Pennsylvania. The names of Pino, McGinnis, Adolph 'Jazz' Maffie, and Henry Baker were frequently mentioned in these rumors; and it was said that they had been with O'Keefe on 'the Big Job.' . . . There was every reason to suspect that O'Keefe felt Pino was turning his back on him now that O'Keefe was in jail. Both O'Keefe and Gusciora had been interviewed on several occasions concerning the Brink's robbery, but they had claimed complete ignorance. In the hope that a wide breach might have developed between the two criminals who were in jail in Pennsylvania and the gang members who were enjoying the luxuries of a free life in Massachusetts, FBI agents again visited Gusciora and O'Keefe. Even in their jail cells, however, they showed no respect for law enforcement."

A federal Grand Jury began hearings in Boston on the Brink's holdup in November 1952—and interviewed ten of the eleven robbers—but reported two months later that it had not found enough evidence to indict anyone.

O'Keefe returned to Boston in 1954, convinced that he had been cheated out of his share of the Brink's money, about $93,000. Maffie confessed to him that he blew it at the track and in card games but O'Keefe wouldn't accept that explanation. On May 18, O'Keefe and a racketeer associate took Vincent Costa, who was Pino's brother–in–law, to a hotel room and held him for several thousand dollars' ransom. Other members of the Brink's gang arranged for O'Keefe to be paid a small part of the ransom, and Costa was released two days later.

"Special agents subsequently interviewed Costa and his wife, Pino and his wife, the racketeer, and O'Keefe," according to the FBI report. "All denied any knowledge of the alleged incident. Nonetheless, several members of the Brink's gang were visibly shaken and appeared to be abnormally worried during the latter part of May and early in June 1954."

On the night of June 5, 1954, Specs was driving to an apartment he rented in Dorchester when a car pulled up next to him and the passenger raked O'Keefe's car with machine gun fire before speeding away. Eleven days later at 3:00 in the morning, as Specky was walking on Adams Street near his apartment, he was attacked again. He ducked behind a parked car, pistol in hand, as machine gun fire blasted at him. His wristwatch was hit by one bullet, cutting him deeply, and another struck him in the chest—deflected away from his heart by a notepad in his pocket. His friend, Johnny Carlson, took him to a doctor to treat the wounds and then took him to a hideout in New Hampshire. The next day, Boston Police arrested a well-known Boston hit man, Elmer "Trigger" Burke, for the attempted murder. In August, Carlson disappeared and was never seen again. On August 28, Burke escaped from the Charles Street Jail during a brazen daylight breakout. Pino was booked on suspicion that he helped in the escape, but was released. Burke was apprehended a year later and executed in 1958 for the 1951 murder of low-level Boston hood Poochy Walsh.

"By the start of 1955, most of Boston believed that the Brink's robbers had indeed pulled off the perfect crime," Schorow wrote. But Specs was in tough shape. He was in prison in Springfield after being arrested on a parole violation. Pino wanted him dead and Trigger Burke was still loose at that time. Specs wrote a letter to Pino and McGinnis demanding his money. They offered him $5,000 but he refused.

The federal statute of limitations had run out, but the FBI still hoped to nab the robbers before the state's statute ran out on January 17, 1956. O'Keefe finally agreed to speak to special agent in charge Edwin Powers. Specs tried to get Gusciora—still behind bars in Pennsylvania—to rat also, but Gus refused to in a phone call between prisons. On January 6, 1956, Specs said to Powers, "All right. What do you want to know?" and spilled the beans. Even his own sister told him he was nuts and asked him why he was doing it.

"Why indeed?" Schorow wrote. "He would not in any sense 'get off.' The FBI made it clear that while they would help him they could not guarantee his release. They could not pay him for his testimony. So what motivated Specky? [FBI agent John] Larkin believes it was pure revenge. O'Keefe believed that he had been double crossed by his former comrades."

On January 11, complaints were issued against the Brink's robbers and on January 12, six of the robbers were arrested. The headline in the *Boston American* read, "Brink's Robbery Solved As Specs O'Keefe Talks."

Richardson and Flaherty avoided capture for four months but were finally arrested on May 16. Banfield had died a year earlier after spending the previous five years in a state of perpetual inebriation. Gusciora died in July from a brain tumor after being transferred from Pennsylvania to Norfolk State Prison.

"He didn't fight it," Schorow wrote. "His best friend had done the unthinkable. He had squealed—and Gus was heartbroken."

Jury selection for the trial started in August. O'Keefe took the stand on September 14, 1956. He testified for seven days. Head defense attorney Paul Smith later derided the prosecution's case in his summary and called O'Keefe "the songbird of Roxbury," but the jury quickly convicted the defendants and Judge Felix Forte sentenced them all to life. Only $51,906 of the Brink's cash was ever recovered, not even a third of what the trial alone cost. The FBI estimates law agencies spent a combined total of $29 million to bring the gang to justice.

Baker and McGinnis both died in prison. All the other convicted gang members were paroled between 1969 and 1971. Pino was the last to walk out of Walpole maximum in July 1971. On October 4, 1973, suffering from emphysema and a variety of other ailments, Pino told author Behn that he still intended to kill Specky, but he suffered a heart attack and died the next day. Maffie and Richardson appeared as extras in 1978's *The Brink's Job,* filmed in Boston and starring Peter Falk as Pino. The screenwriters turned the heist into a comedy and portrayed the gang as happy-go-lucky caricatures.

"Still, Bostonians welcomed the opening of the movie as if it were a homage to Paul Revere's ride or the Boston Tea Party," Schorow wrote. "On Monday, December 5, 1978, Boston Mayor Kevin White standing on the steps of City Hall, flanked by the filmmakers and Jazz Maffie and Sandy Richardson, declared 'Brink's Week' in Boston."

Specky remained isolated in the East Cambridge Jail for four years after the trial. He had little contact with other prisoners. He was released in June 1960 and relocated to California under the name Paul Williams. He worked a series of jobs, including chauffeur and houseman for actor Cary Grant, and Considine paid him at least $1,500 for his as-told-to story. Specky longed to return to Boston, but his wife would not even let him in her house. Some members of the gang never forgave him. In a 1975 interview with the *Boston Globe,* a bitter Vinnie Geagan called O'Keefe "a dirty, weak son of a bitch."

Specky himself told reporters that he came to regret being a stool pigeon, but that his desire for revenge drove him to rat. He was arrested four times for drunk driving in California between 1967 and 1971.

"Something inside me won't let me enjoy anything I do," Specs told the *Boston Globe's* Richard Connolly fourteen months before he died of natural causes in Beverly Hills in March 1976. "I blame it all on what I did. . . . I've done penance for too many years."

CHAPTER 17

Albert DeSalvo
The Boston Strangler

A nyone who lived in Boston or its suburbs in the sweltering summer of 1962 remembers the abject fear that smothered the city like a hot blanket that season.

A killer was on the loose—a killer who brutally raped and strangled older, single women, tying neat bows around their necks with their own nylons and underwear, often leaving them in odd sexual poses to be discovered by relatives, roommates, or the police officers who opened their apartment doors.

The man soon to be known as "The Boston Strangler" claimed his first victim on June 14. In a brief story on June 15, the *Boston Globe* reported: "An attractive divorcee was found strangled in her third-floor apartment at 77 Gainsborough St., Back Bay, at 7:45 last night."

Anna Slesers was a fifty-five-year-old Latvian seamstress who lived alone in an apartment near Symphony Hall. She was discovered by her twenty-three-year-old son, her blue bathrobe ripped open, the sash tightened around her neck with a big bow. She had been sexually assaulted, possibly with an object. Police questioned eight men, but all were released.

The second victim died two weeks later, although no connection was made at the time because eighty-five-year-old Mary Mullen died not by strangling, but by a heart attack when the would-be strangler grabbed her from behind. Mullen was found on her sofa in her apartment on Commonwealth Avenue.

Two days later, the killer struck twice. Nina Nichols, sixty-eight, who also lived on "Comm Ave," as Bostonians call it, was found on her bedroom floor, her pink robe torn from the waist down and two stockings tied around her neck. She had been sexually assaulted with a wine bottle. Two days later in the suburb of Lynn on the North Shore, Helen Blake, a sixty-five-year-old nurse, was discovered face down in her apartment, the bottoms of her pajamas on the floor, a stocking and a bra tied around her neck. She also had been sexually assaulted. Police said she, like Nichols, had been murdered on June 30.

"Another Silk Stocking Murder, Two Women Slain the Same Day," screamed one Boston headline on July 2. Strangler hysteria was on and the "Olde Towne" would never be the same. Hysteria kicked into high gear on August 19, when the body of seventy-five-year-old Ida Irga was discovered in her fifth-floor Beacon Hill apartment, lying on her back, her night robe torn up the front, exposing her naked body. Her legs were spread with her feet locked between the rungs of chairs as if she were undergoing a gynecological exam.

"As the victims were discovered one by one over the steamy summer months, a bone-chilling fear, beyond anything known before or since in Boston, descended on the city and far around it," Loretta McLaughlin, who covered the crimes for the *Boston Record American,* wrote in a *Boston Globe* story thirty years later. "The slain bodies were bizarrely positioned and strangely manipulated sexually, their bruised and swollen necks garishly decorated with large, looping bows. For a seemingly endless 18 months, and eventual 13 deaths, the terror of the Boston Strangler cast a shadow on the daily routines of everyone who lived and worked in the city."

The fear was as palpable as the Hub's humidity. Few women ventured out on the streets alone, day or night. Many single women moved in with friends. Police stations were bombarded with calls from worried families when their daughters or mothers didn't answer their phones. Hardware stores sold out of deadbolts before they could be stocked on shelves. Every dog the Animal Rescue League received—no matter the size or age—was adopted the next day.

"I was 10, and I remember it vividly," Jack McDevitt, a professor at Northeastern University's College of Criminal Justice told the *Globe* in 2002. "The level of fear was phenomenal."

Despite the heightened fear, no victim's apartment showed signs of forced entry.

The women were always dead or unconscious before the Strangler molested them. Another victim, Jane Sullivan, sixty-seven, of Dorchester, had been killed on the same day as Ida Irga, but her body was not found for more than a week. She was strangled with two nylon stockings tied together. Her killer had left her in the bathtub in a kneeling position. At that point, all of the Strangler's victims were older women. Of the next eight, though, six were twenty-three or younger.

On December 5, a roommate discovered twenty-year-old hospital technician Sophie Clark in their Huntington Avenue apartment, lying on her back, legs spread, strangled by a stocking and petticoat intertwined. On the carpet near her body, police found semen stains. On New Year's Eve, a janitor on Park Drive called by an anxious employer discovered pregnant Patricia Bissette, twenty-three, strangled with three nylon stockings and a blouse.

The killing continued in 1963. Mary Brown, sixty-nine, was found in her Lawrence apartment, raped, strangled, her head bashed in, a kitchen fork still stuck in her chest.

Victim number ten was Boston University music major Beverly Samans, twenty-three, found naked on her bed in Cambridge in May, stabbed sixteen times, her hands tied behind her back, and two silk scarves and a nylon stocking around her neck.

The strangler—but not the fear—took the summer off. He struck again on September 8 in Salem. A neighbor found Evelyn Corbin, fifty-eight, on her bed with two stockings wrapped around her neck. She had been raped. Two months later, on the same day Massachusetts's favorite son, President John F. Kennedy, was assassinated, the Strangler claimed victim number twelve. After Sunday School teacher Joann Graff, twenty-three, failed to show up for services at Redeemer Lutheran Church two days later, police found her nude body with two nylon stockings and a leotard knotted around her neck.

The Strangler was almost done. On January 4, 1964, nineteen-year-old Mary Sullivan's roommates returned to their Charles

Street apartment from a shopping trip and thought Mary was sleeping. A little while later they decided to wake her but discovered Mary was dead, two pink scarves and a stocking tied around her neck in a bow, a broom handle inside her, and a card that said "Happy New Year" propped up against her foot.

Then, "the stranglings stopped as suddenly and mysteriously as they had begun," McLaughlin wrote. The terror did not. State Attorney General Edward W. Brooke, later elected to the US Senate, established the Boston Strangler Bureau. He also hired a police detail to guard his wife and two teenage daughters. The Strangler Bureau, which included hundreds of local, state, and federal law agents, part of the largest manhunt in the history of the state, could produce no credible suspects. Brooke even consented to hiring Peter Hurkos, a well-known Dutch psychic. Private groups paid for Hurkos's services and expenses, but he also produced no suspects.

Then, in November 1964, famed attorney F. Lee Bailey heard from one of his clients, a brutal murderer named George Nassar.

Nassar was being held in the state's Bridgewater Center for the Treatment of Sexually Dangerous Persons, awaiting trial for the execution-style slaying of an Andover gas station attendant. A wiry, thirty-three-year-old married guy named Albert DeSalvo, who had been arrested for rape on October 27 by Cambridge police, had been sent to Bridgewater for psychiatric evaluation and he shared a cell with Nassar.

Nassar told Bailey that his cellmate had confessed to him that he was the Boston Strangler. Bailey alerted police that he might have a strong suspect for them and they provided the lawyer with some information about the stranglings that had never been publicized. Already nationally famous because of the Dr. Sam Sheppard case, Bailey went to visit DeSalvo with a Dictaphone on March 6 and found him courteous and knowledgeable. When Bailey, and subsequently police, interviewed DeSalvo, he revealed details about the killings—the color of appliances, the way a door opened, articles in apartments, that buttons had popped off a blouse—that had never been made public.

They had their man—or did they? Some thought that Nassar, who had an IQ of 150 and was considered a strong suspect, might have told DeSalvo details and that DeSalvo perversely claimed credit. Bailey, however, believed DeSalvo.

"I became certain that the man sitting in that dimly lit room with me was the Boston Strangler," Bailey later wrote. "Anyone experienced in interrogation learns to recognize the difference between a man speaking from life and a man telling a story that he either has made up or has gotten from another person. DeSalvo gave me every indication that he was speaking from life. He wasn't trying to recall words; he was recalling scenes he had actually experienced. He could bring back the most inconsequential details . . . the color of a rug, the content of a photograph, the condition of a piece of furniture. . . . Then, as if he were watching a videotape replay, he would describe what had happened, usually as unemotionally as if he were describing a trip to the supermarket."

Bailey asked DeSalvo why he would want to confess. DeSalvo told him. "I know I'm going to have to spend the rest of my life locked up somewhere. I just hope it's a hospital, and not a hole like this [Bridgewater]. But if I could tell my story to somebody who could write it, maybe I could make some money for my family."

Detectives from the Boston Strangler Bureau interviewed DeSalvo over the next six months and produced more than fifty hours of tapes and two thousand pages of transcription. He said he always posed as someone sent by the building superintendent and that sometimes it took some cajoling, but the women always let him in. DeSalvo's confession convinced officials they had their man.

"I just drove in and out of streets and ended up wherever I ended up," DeSalvo confessed. "I never knew where I was going. I never knew what I was doing. That's why you never nailed me, because you never knew where I was going to strike and I didn't either."

In defending DeSalvo on the rape charges in January 1967, Bailey introduced the confession, hoping it would persuade a jury that DeSalvo was insane. "The basic strategy was . . . simple: I would attempt to use the thirteen murders he had committed as the Boston Strangler to show the extent of his insanity," Bailey wrote. "To do this, I would try to get both his confession and its corroboration by police into evidence. Certainly the problem was unusual: I wanted the right to defend a man for robbery and assault by proving that he had committed thirteen murders."

The strategy failed and after an eight-day trial the jury found DeSalvo guilty, not insane, and he was sentenced to life in prison for the rapes. By now, though, the whole world had a face to put with the Boston Strangler.

It was a handsome Italian face, with a prominent nose, and DeSalvo had a way with women. Prior to the stranglings, DeSalvo had admitted to being the "Measuring Man," who knocked on doors in Boston and Cambridge, claiming that he was looking for models who would be paid $40 an hour. Police reported they were amazed by how many women were willing to admit him to their home, take off their clothes, and even make love to him.

"I'm not good-looking, I'm not educated, but I was able to put something over on high-class people," he explained in his confession. "They were all college kids and I never had anything in my life and I outsmarted them."

The rape that sent him to Bridgewater was one in a series of post-strangling "Green Man" rapes in southern New England, in which the victims told police the rapist wore a green handyman uniform. In his confession, DeSalvo later estimated he had raped two thousand women during his life.

Born September 3, 1931, DeSalvo grew up in Chelsea, a working-class city next to Boston and one of the poorest communities in the state. His father, Frank DeSalvo, was a plumber and vicious drunk who often beat his wife Charlotte and young Albert, his three brothers and two sisters.

"I saw my father knock my mother's teeth out and then break every one of her fingers. I must have been seven," he told police in his confession. "He smashed me once across the back with a pipe. I just didn't move fast enough. He once sold me and my two sisters

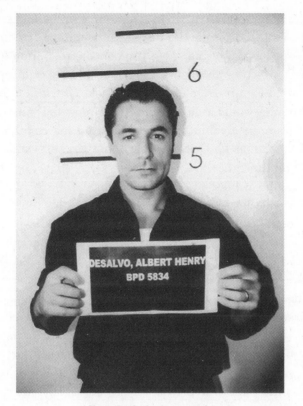

Albert DeSalvo's mug shot

for nine dollars, sold us to some farmer in Maine" for four months as slaves.

Frank DeSalvo often brought home prostitutes and had sex with them in front of his wife and children. He also taught Albert to shoplift. Albert began torturing animals, putting stray dogs and cats in crates and letting them claw each other to death. When Albert was twelve, he was arrested for beating up a paperboy and stealing $2.85 from him. He also broke into a neighbor's apartment and stole jewelry. He was placed in the Lyman School for Boys in Westboro. He was let out after a few months, but was quickly returned there after stealing a car. His mother divorced Frank, but when his new stepfather started beating him too, Albert quit school after his ninth grade graduation in 1948. That summer, he and one of his brothers washed dishes in the restaurant of a Cape Cod motel.

"He spent most of his spare time on the roof, from where he could look directly into some of the rooms and see couples making love," Gerold Frank wrote in his 1966 book, *The Boston Strangler*. "Watching, he would relieve himself by repeated masturbation. He had been an involuntary voyeur during his childhood: since puberty voyeurism had become a regular means of sexual stimulation and fulfillment."

During his confession, DeSalvo claimed to have an insatiable sex drive, one that required satisfaction five or six times a day.

In the fall of 1948, the seventeen-year-old DeSalvo joined the Army. He served from 1948 until 1956, mostly in Germany, where he met Irmgard Beck. They married four years later. They had two children, a son and a daughter who was born with a crippling pelvic disease. DeSalvo later claimed Irmgard's subsequent reluctance to satisfy him for fear of becoming pregnant played a role in his drive to rape. While still in the service, DeSalvo was arrested in New Jersey for carnal abuse of a nine-year-old girl, but the charge was never prosecuted at the request of her parents. He was also busted down to private for disobeying an officer, but still received an honorable discharge.

Once he left the service, DeSalvo worked a series of factory, construction, and handyman jobs. He was arrested several times for breaking and entering and robbery, each time receiving a suspended sentence. After yet another B&E arrest in March 1961, DeSalvo admitted to being "The Measuring Man." The court sent him to Westboro State Psychiatric Hospital, where he was diagnosed as a sociopath. He then was tried on the B&E charge and for assault and battery. The judge sent him to the Billerica House of Correction for two years but he was released early and was back on the street in April 1962. Two months later, the Strangler claimed his first victim.

DeSalvo was never charged or tried for the thirteen stranglings he confessed to having committed. In a deal made between Bailey and Brooke, execution was taken off the table, the confessions could not be used, and the police were without corroborating evidence. His other convictions for rape, however, ensured DeSalvo would stay in prison for life. In February 1967 he threw Massachusetts into a panic once again and prompted a massive manhunt when he escaped from Bridgewater with two other inmates. He turned himself in the next day in Lynn. He was transferred to the maximum-security prison known at the time as Walpole State Prison, now MCI-Cedar Junction, where he made women's jewelry—his specialty chokers—in the crafts shop. Six years later, on November 26, 1973, he was stabbed to death while sleeping in the infirmary. The door of his cell had been left open. No one was ever found guilty of his murder.

"DeSalvo is one of the least understood of all modern multiple murderers," Elliot Leyton, a Canadian college professor and serial killer expert, wrote in his 1986 book, *Hunting Humans.* "He murdered 13 women and then, just as suddenly [stopped]. He was not an intelligent man, and he only dimly perceived his own motivations—which had to be teased out of him by police and psychiatric interrogators. . . . DeSalvo cooperated with the inquiry in every way, but the results were impoverished both by his own bewilderment at what he had done and by his tendency to revel in his center-stage position in what he called, 'the biggest story of the century.'"

Questions still linger. Author Susan Kelly in her 1995 book, *The Boston Stranglers: The Public Conviction of Albert DeSalvo and the True Story of Eleven Shocking Murders,* argued that there is no chance one man committed all the murders. She and many others point to the dissimilarities in the victims—Sophie Clark was the only African American, the ages varied from nineteen to eighty-five, the method of killing ranged from almost gentle to brutal and bloody. Mary Sullivan's nephew Casey Sherman cowrote *A Rose for Mary: The Hunt for the Boston Strangler* in 2003, making the case that DeSalvo did not commit her murder. His family and the DeSalvo family had agreed to have her body exhumed two years earlier and forensics revealed no trace of Albert's DNA on her body.

Bailey remained convinced DeSalvo was indeed the Strangler. Many others close to the case agree.

"They got the right man," Frank Corsetti, a *Record American* reporter who had covered the stranglings, told the *Globe* in 2002. "Why? Various things DeSalvo knew, things never published. One involved Patricia Bissette. She lived in an apartment in Back Bay, and DeSalvo told police that after he strangled her, he noticed the door to her apartment was in violation of the city code. Now, don't forget, he was a handyman. He told the cops that instead of opening in, the door opened out. They went back and checked, and he was right. In another case, Jane Sullivan, she was found in the bathtub, and a broom had been inserted in her. DeSalvo told police the faucets on her tub were labeled wrong—the one that read 'Hot' gave cold and the 'Cold' gave hot. They checked. It was true."

Ed Brooke, the man in charge of the Boston Strangler investigation, is no longer certain DeSalvo was his intended target. Now retired in Florida, Brooke told the *Globe* in 2012 that the details provided by DeSalvo were uncannily correct but, "I'll probably go to my grave not knowing for sure."

CHAPTER 18

Charles M. Stuart
"From ultimate victim to ultimate villain"

On the night of October 23, 1989, Massachusetts State Police dispatcher Gary McLaughlin picked up a 911 line.

"My wife's been shot," the caller, twenty-nine-year-old Charles M. "Chuck" Stuart, said. "I've been shot."

"Where are you?" the dispatcher asked.

"I have no idea," Stuart answered. He said he and his wife Carol, seven months pregnant, had just left a birthing class at Boston's Brigham and Women's Hospital.

For a frantic thirteen minutes, the dispatcher tried to help Stuart figure out where he was. Stuart drove a few blocks and when he started to pass out, the dispatcher told him to put down his windows. Cruisers in the area intermittently sounded their sirens and, by the increasing volume coming through Stuart's car phone, they were able to zero in on the 1987 Toyota Cressida. The couple was rushed to different nearby hospitals—Carol Stuart back to Brigham and Women's, Charles Stuart to Boston City.

"Reading Woman Dies After Shooting in Car: Husband, Baby Termed Critical," screamed the *Boston Globe* headline on October 25.

No one knew then that the "Charles Stuart case" as it would come to be called, would be one of the strangest murder cases in the city's long history. It would also add yet another troubled chapter to the Athens of America's uneven racial chronicles.

No one—not the police or politicians or the media—at first suspected the case was anything but what Charles Stuart claimed it was: A white suburban couple awaiting the arrival of their first child was robbed and shot by a black man during a carjacking in a tough neighborhood. Dispatcher McLaughlin, lauded for the innovative way he helped police find the couple, was even quoted as saying, "In my opinion, Mr. Stuart is the hero in all this."

Newspapers dutifully reported what police told them.

"Late Monday night, doctors at Brigham and Women's Hospital delivered an eight weeks' premature baby boy from the 33-year-old woman," the *Globe* wrote in that first-day front-page story. "Carol Stuart was pronounced dead about 3 a.m. . . . The Stuarts were accosted by a gunman at the corner of Huntington Avenue and Francis Street, apparently while waiting for a stoplight, police said. The attacker forced them to drive to an undetermined location several blocks away, robbed them of $100 cash and their watches, and then shot the woman once in the head and her husband in the stomach before fleeing."

At the scene, Charles Stuart had described the attacker as a five-foot-ten black man about thirty years old, with a wispy beard and raspy voice. Stuart told the police the assailant saw his car phone and said "I think you're 5-0," street slang for police, before shooting them. "There's no question the perpetrator thought they were police officers," one investigator told the *Globe*. Detectives also told the newspapers they were convinced the gunman lived in or routinely committed crimes around the Mission Hill housing project, where the shooting occurred. "Some police sources believe the assailant probably has committed several similar robberies by jumping into stopped cars at intersections," the *Globe* reported.

The Stuarts' baby boy, Christopher, deprived of oxygen as his mother died, also died seventeen days later, "shortly after his father cradled him in his arms one last time," Kevin Cullen wrote in a *Globe* retrospective five years later. "Stuart cried as the nurses and homicide detectives looked on."

Boston, and the entire country, was transfixed by the horror of the shooting, its randomness, and its racial overtones.

"The white-controlled media in the northeast and across the nation quickly fell for the story and 'apotheosized the couple as

The case ended here when Charles Stuart jumped off the Tobin Bridge.

starry-eyed lovers out of Camelot cut down by an urban savage,'" Joe Feagin wrote in his 2001 book, *White Racism: The Basics*.

Massachusetts Republican Party leaders immediately urged reinstatement of the death penalty. Boston Mayor Raymond Flynn and police commanders promised an around-the-clock investigation until the killer—the "animal," Flynn said—was caught. More than one hundred detectives descended on the Mission Hill housing project to interview and search residents. Chief of Detectives Joseph V. Saia Jr. soon said the list of suspects had been narrowed down to a few, but when a week passed without an arrest, a group of businessmen offered a reward of $15,000 for information. A homeless man was detained for three weeks and then released as police aggressively continued to stop and search young black men in the Mission Hill area. In December police leaked that Willie Bennett, another Mission Hill resident who was being held in a separate robbery, was their prime suspect and that one of his relatives had heard him brag he was the shooter.

"One of the best examples of an inappropriate response to violence was the highly publicized 1990 case," Deborah Prothrow-Stith and Howard Spivak wrote in their 2004 book, *Murder Is No Accident: Understanding and Preventing Youth Violence in America*. "The political response from City Hall was dramatic and extensive. Random searches were instituted in inner-city neighborhoods, and all the misguided stereotypes relating to race and youth were evoked."

From his hospital bed, Charles Stuart wrote a passage to be read by a friend at his wife's funeral, in which his brothers Matthew and Michael served as pallbearers.

"In our souls, we must forgive this sinner because He would too," Stuart wrote. "Good night sweet wife, my love. God has called you to his side. . . . Now you sleep away from me. I will never again know the feeling of your hand in mine, but will always feel you. I miss you and I love you."

Charles Stuart would put pen to paper again on January 4. He left a note on the passenger seat of the 1990 Nissan Maxima he had bought with insurance money just two days earlier, less than a month after his release from the hospital, just seventy-three days after his wife's death, and less than a week after he identified Bennett as the shooter in a police lineup. Stuart parked the new car on the lower deck of the Tobin Bridge, popped the hood up, put the flashers on, and then leaped over the railing and down into the water where the Mystic River meets Boston Harbor.

"When the police found his car at a few minutes before 7, they were not sure, until they found his submerged body, that this was not another hoax," *New York Times* reporter Fox Butterfield wrote in his story, "A Boston Tragedy" eleven days later.

Stuart's short missive, written on notepaper from the Sheraton Tara in Braintree where he had spent his last night alive, said in part, "I love my family . . . The last four months have been real hell . . . all the allegations have taken all my strength. . . .Whatever this new accusation is, it has beaten me."

It did not contain a confession. Police didn't need one—they had already obtained that the day before from Matthew Stuart, Charles's youngest brother. Matthew had told police that Charles had planned and executed the robbery and shooting of Carol and then shot himself to cover it up. Matthew, twenty-three, also admitted he met his brother on Mission Hill immediately after the shooting to take the gun and Carol's jewelry. Matthew claimed he didn't know Carol was dead or that Charles was shot when his brother gave him a Gucci bag with the gun and jewelry in it. Until he learned of the shooting hours later, he said he thought it was all an elaborate scheme to collect insurance money on the stolen jewelry. (In reality, Charles Stuart had several life insurance policies on Carol worth a total of more than a half million dollars). Matthew admitted to later throwing the .38 snub-nosed revolver used to kill his sister-in-law into the Pines River in Revere. Suffolk County District Attorney Newman A. Flanagan told detectives to find and arrest Charles Stuart for the murder of his wife and child. By the time they found him, he was dead, sunken in the Mystic River.

"Matt knew from the outset, or had reason to suspect, that the official version was not what happened," Matthew Stuart's attorney, John Perenyi, told reporters after he and his client met with Flanagan. "But when his brother fingered Mr. Bennett, that pushed him over the brink. . . . It was a tough decision. It's not easy to turn state's evidence on your brother."

Matthew Stuart and a friend were indicted for their roles in the insurance fraud attempt and murder cover-up. Matthew pleaded guilty and served two and a half years in prison. Revere police arrested him on drug charges shortly after his release in 1995. He died at forty-five years old of a cocaine overdose in Heading Home, a homeless shelter in Cambridge, in 2011.

Charles and Matthew grew up in a small red Cape Cod–style house on dead-end Lowe Street in Revere, a working-class city of about fifty thousand people—almost all white and less than 3 percent black—that borders on East Boston. Charles, the oldest boy and Matthew the youngest, shared bedrooms with two other brothers. Family and friends called Charles "Chuck." Their father, mother, and two half sisters from their father's previous marriage also lived there. The father, Charlie Stuart, was an insurance salesman who moonlighted as a bartender at a local pub, popular around town and always ready to lend a hand at a local fund-raiser.

Chuck Stuart was born on December 18, 1959. He and his siblings walked just a few blocks to elementary school at the Church of the Immaculate Conception. His younger brothers adored him, but Chuck, tall, athletic, and handsome, developed early aspirations of a richer life beyond his blue-collar background.

"Although friends remember Stuart as a happy, if quiet, child, some say that as he grew older he talked little about his family, apparently embarrassed about his modest beginnings," *Boston Globe* reporter Sally Jacobs wrote.

Stuart studied culinary arts at Northeast Metropolitan Regional Vocational High School in Wakefield and became obsessed with someday owning his own restaurant. When he graduated in 1977, Stuart took a job as a cook at an Italian restaurant in Revere, the Driftwood. He began dating Carol DiMaiti, an outgoing Boston College student who was the daughter of a Driftwood bartender and working as a waitress there.

In 1981 Stuart tired of cooking and applied to Kakas & Sons, a fur store on Boston's upscale Newbury Street. He was hired and in less than five years became the manager. Carol had become a lawyer by then and the Stuarts could afford to move to a suburban house with a swimming pool and Jacuzzi.

"To all appearances, things were going well for Chuck and Carol," Butterfield wrote in his *Times* piece in 1990. "They got married in 1985, bought a house in Reading, a much more affluent town than Revere, and after Carol became pregnant last year, they began buying baby clothes and furniture. Carol was due in December."

Appearances can be deceiving. On his resume, Chuck claimed he went to Brown University on a football scholarship but had left the Ivy League School and finished his degree at Salem State College. In fact, he never even applied to Brown and only went to Salem State for two months in 1979. Investigators later learned that Stuart had been upset that Carol refused to get an abortion because he was worried she would not return to work after a baby was born. They also learned that Stuart had been staying out late and had developed an interest in a beautiful twenty-two-year-old woman who worked with him. A friend, David F. MacLean, later told Boston station WCVB-TV that Stuart had asked him in September for help in killing Carol.

"Friends, relatives and law-enforcement officials now say Mr. Stuart may have been consumed by his own rapid financial success," Butterfield wrote. " He was a man who had gone from being a short-order cook in a bar a decade ago, making $4 an hour, to the manager of a fur salon on Newbury Street, earning more than $100,000 last year.

"It was a long journey from his hometown of Revere, a blue-collar community best known for its dog track and neighborhood bars, to the affluent environs of Newbury Street, with its fashionable boutiques and crowded restaurants in Boston's Back Bay."

Stuart finally enlisted his youngest brother in his nefarious plot to cash in on the insurance policies. They even did a "dry run" in Mission Hill the day before, although Matthew always maintained he did not know murder would be involved.

Charles Stuart's heinous crime and the city's reaction once again ripped open scars on century-deep racial wounds in Boston. Though known as a city of great progressive thinkers, fine cultural institutions, and many of the country's greatest universities, the "Cradle of Liberty" has long battled an undercurrent of animosity between blacks and whites, particularly the Irish working-class majority who still smart from their own nineteenth-century mistreatment at the hands of upper-class abolitionists. The Red Sox were the last major league baseball team to put a black player on the field. In the 1950s, Boston Celtic great Bill Russell called Boston, "a flea market of racism" after vandals ransacked his home and wrote racial epithets on the walls. In the 1970s the old hatreds resulted in weeks of violence in Irish South Boston when officials tried to enforce school integration through forced busing. The Stuart case once again ripped that scar open. Black leaders pointed out that the murder of blacks in Boston—even of a fourteen-year-old boy or young mother—received scant media attention. They said police consciously ignored that 90 percent of crimes involve people of the same race and the most likely suspect in a murder is generally the victim's spouse.

"Since black males have become racially coded symbols for pathological, criminal behavior, the Stuart [story] found millions of white believers," Michael Eric Dyson wrote in his 1996 book *Race Rules: Navigating the Color Line.* "Such beliefs about black males are subtle updates of an ancient belief about black men as beasts and sexual predators."

Mea culpas from Boston officials and the Boston media did little to abate the criticism.

"The most powerful visions of parental failure, at-risk youth, and family collapse in the past few years have been tinted black," Stephanie Coontz wrote in *The Way We Never Were: American Families and the Nostalgia Trap* in 1992. "'Wilding' gangs; crazed cocaine addicts; macho men lacking the slightest shred of decency toward women and children: these images so pervaded the mass media that in 1989, Charles Stuart of Boston believed he could get away with murdering his pregnant wife by blaming a black mugger. His ploy almost succeeded: Public pressure to catch the criminal reached near-hysteria and police swarmed over black sections of town, strip-searching men and boys on street corners, until they settled on an ex-convict who fit the category."

No one came out of the Stuart case feeling good. The DiMaiti family oozed bitterness over Matthew and other members of the Stuart family who knew what Chuck had done. "Can you believe that they came over to our house to comfort my parents?" Carol's brother Carl DiMaiti said in an interview on WLVI-TV. "It is just mind-boggling that they could sit with us, or allow us to visit Chuck, to cry over him and pray for his recovery, knowing that Chuck was responsible for what happened to Carol." Boston's black community once again felt the sting of negative stereotyping. Boston Police felt they had been unfairly made the scapegoats in an almost perfectly planned crime. "People forget how serious [Stuart's stomach] wounds were," Police Commissioner Paul Evans told the *Globe*. "I mean, the guy almost died." After Stuart's suicide, black community leaders organized a boycott of the *Boston Globe* for being far too willing to assign the murder to a black man.

"*Globe* columnist Ellen Goodman publicly admitted that her newspaper had been wrong in its facts but defended its coverage by saying that, although newspaper reporters had chased down 'every' lead, the information they received had been deficient and that what they had written was correct at the time of publication even though events proved the story wrong," Tom Koch wrote in his 1991 book *Journalism for the 21st Century*. "*Newsweek,* which had also covered the original event, joined in criticism of press coverage of the Stuart shooting and the failure of Boston reporters to fulfill a 'primary job description'—'skepticism'—and consider the possibility that the surviving victim, Charles Stuart, was in fact the perpetrator of the crime."

On January 3, 1990, Kevin Cullen had been on the team of *Globe* reporters covering Stuart's suicide. "By leaping to his death from the Tobin Bridge," the reporters wrote the next day, "Stuart completed his sudden transformation from ultimate victim to ultimate villain." In his October 23, 1994, retrospective, Cullen noted the *Boston Globe* had published more than six hundred stories about the Stuart case since the crime. "Portrayed as the ultimate urban nightmare for suburbanites, the story attracted national and international media," he wrote. "Today, the Stuart case reverberates in a city that seems to trip over itself whenever race is the issue."

However, Dr. Robert Coles, a psychiatrist at Harvard University, told the *New York Times* the Stuart case was not so much about Boston's history of racial animosity, its police, or the media, as it was about Charles Stuart's own devious and calculating personality.

"'In most psychopaths there is cruelty and callousness,' Dr. Coles said, "but Stuart outdoes that."

Bibliography

Cotton Mather

Gragg, Larry. *The Salem Witch Crisis*. Westport, CT: Praeger, 1992.

Hall, Timothy L. "Cotton Mather." *American Religious Leaders, American Biographies*. New York: Facts On File, Inc., 2002.

Lutz, Norma Jean. *Cotton Mather: Author, Clergyman and Scholar*. Philadelphia: Chelsea House Publications, 2000.

Mather, Cotton. *Memorable Providences, Relating to Witchcrafts and Possessions*. London: 1689.

Mather, Cotton and Increase Mather. *The Wonders of the Invisible World: Being an Account of the Tryals of Several Witches Lately Executed in New England*. London: John Russell Smith, 1862.

Sifakis, Carl. "Cotton Mather and the Salem Witch Trials." *The Encyclopedia of American Crime*. 2nd ed. New York: Facts On File, Inc., 2001.

Silverman, Kenneth. *The Life and Times of Cotton Mather*. New York: Harper & Row, 1984.

Starkey, Marion L. *The Devil in Massachusetts*. New York: Alfred A. Knopf Inc., 1949.

Wendell, Barrett. *Cotton Mather: The Puritan Priest*. New York: Dodd & Mead, 1891.

Thomas Hutchinson

Bailyn, Bernard. *The Ordeal of Thomas Hutchinson*. Cambridge, MA: Belknap Press of Harvard University, 1974.

Hosmer, James K. *The Life of Thomas Hutchinson, Royal Governor of the Province of Massachusetts Bay*. Boston: Houghton Mifflin and Company, 1896.

Hutchinson, Thomas and John Hutchinson. *The History of the Province of Massachusetts Bay: From 1749 to 1774*. London: John Murray, Albemarle Street, 1828.

McCullough, David. *John Adams*. New York: Simon & Schuster, 2001.

Rutland, Robert A. *Clio's Favorites: Leading Historians of the United States, 1945–2000*. Columbia: University of Missouri Press, 2000.

Ward, Adolphus & William Trent, et al. *The Cambridge History of English and American Literature*. New York: G.P. Putnam's Sons, 1907.

Benjamin Church

Fischer, David H. *Paul Revere's Ride*. New York: Oxford University Press, 1994.

Forbes, Esther H. *Paul Revere and the World He Lived In*. New York: Houghton Mifflin, 1942.

Hosmer, James K. *The Life of Thomas Hutchinson, Royal Governor of the Province of Massachusetts Bay*. Boston: Houghton Mifflin and Company, 1896.

Middlekauff, Robert. *The Glorious Cause: The American Revolution, 1763–1789*. New York: Oxford University Press, 1985.

Potter, David and Gordon Thomas. *The Colonial Idiom*. Carbondale: Southern Illinois University Press, 1970.

Tudor, William and James Warren. *Letters to John Adams, 1775*. Massachusetts Historical Society digital collection. Accessed September 12, 2012. www.masshist.org/publications/.

Valcourt, Richard and Arthur Hulnick. *Fixing the Spy Machine: Preparing American Intelligence for the Twenty-First Century*. Westport, CT: Praeger, 1999.

Wood, Sylvanus. 1858 affidavit included in "Battle at Lexington Green, 1775." 2011. Accessed September 5, 2012. www.eyewitnesstohistory.com.

John W. Webster

American Experience at PBS.org. "Murder at Harvard." Accessed September 20, 2012. www.pbs.org/wgbh/amex/murder/index.html.

Bemis, George. *Report of the Case of John W. Webster . . . Including the Hearing on the Petition for a Writ of Error, the Prisoner's Confessional Statements and Application for a Commutation of Sentence.* Boston: Charles C. Little and James Brown, 1850.

Irving, H. B. *A Book of Remarkable Criminals.* New York: George H. Doran Company, 1918.

Levy, Leonard W. *The Law of the Commonwealth and Chief Justice Shaw.* New York: Oxford University Press, 1986.

London Times. "The Boston Murder." December 27, 1849.

Ramsland, Katherine. *Beating the Devil's Game, A History of Forensic Science and Criminal Investigation.* New York: Berkley Publishing Group, 2007.

———. "George Parkman." Crime Library at Trutv.com. Accessed September 15, 2012. www.trutv.com/library/crime/notorious_murders/classics/george_parkman/1.html.

Schama, Simon. *Dead Certainties, Unwarranted Speculations.* New York: Knopf, 1991.

Stone, James W. *Report of the Trial of Prof. John W. Webster, Indicted for the Murder of Dr. George Parkman before the Supreme Judicial Court of Massachusetts.* Boston: Phillips, Sampson and Company, 1950.

A. Bronson Alcott

Brown, Amy Belding. "Amos Bronson Alcott 1799–1888." American Transcendentalist Web. Accessed May 5, 2012. http://transcendentalism.tamu.edu/authors/alcott/.

Francis, Richard. *Fruitlands: The Alcott Family and Their Search for Utopia.* New Haven: Yale University Press, 2010.

Freeman, Jan. "Don't Say It: The Art of Dodging Bad Words." *Boston Globe,* February 13, 2011.

Holbrook, Stewart. "The Beard of Joseph Palmer." *American Scholar* (Autumn 1944): 455–458.

Interview with Thomas Palmer. *Boston Daily Globe,* 1884.

McCuskey, Dorothy. *Bronson Alcott, Teacher.* New York: The Macmillan Company, 1940.

Sanborn, F. B. and William T. Harris. *A. Bronson Alcott, His Life and Philosophy.* New York: Biblo and Tannen, 1893. Reprint: 1965.

Sears, Clara Endicott. *Bronson Alcott's Fruitlands with Transcendental Wild Oats by Louisa May Alcott.* Cambridge and Boston: Houghton Mifflin and The Riverside Press, 1915.

Swift, Lindsay. *Brook Farm: Its Members, Scholars and Visitors.* New York: Macmillan, 1900.

www.alcott.net. A treasure trove of information and documents about Alcott.

Joshua V. Himes

Abanes, Richard. *End-Time Visions: The Road to Armageddon?* New York: Four Walls, Eight Windows, 1998.

Bliss, Sylvester. *Memoirs of William Miller.* Boston: Joshua V. Himes, 1853. Reprint, Berrien Springs, MI: Andrews University Press, 2006.

Brekus, Catherine A. *Strangers & Pilgrims: Female Preaching in America, 1740–1845.* Chapel Hill: University of North Carolina Press, 1998.

Conklin, Paul K. *American Originals: Homemade Varieties of Christianity.* Chapel Hill: University of North Carolina Press, 1997.

Dick, Everett. *Founders of the Message.* Washington, DC: Review and Herald Publishers, 1938. Accessed July 16, 2012. www.maranathmedia.com.au.

Morgan, David. *Protestants & Pictures: Religion, Visual Culture and the Age of American Mass Production.* New York: Oxford University Press, 1999.

O'Leary, Stephen D. *Arguing the Apocalypse: A Theory of Millennial Rhetoric.* New York: Oxford University Press, 1998.

Sears, Clara Endicott. *Days of Delusion.* Cambridge, MA: The Riverside Press, 1924.

Henry J. Gardner

Anbinder, Tyler. *Nativism and Slavery: The Northern Know Nothings and the Politics of the 1850s.* New York: Oxford University Press, 1992.

Beatty, Jack. *The Rascal King: The Life and Times of James Michael Curley, 1874–1958.* Reading, MA: Addison-Wesley, 1992.

Bennett, David H. *The Party of Fear: From Nativist Movements to the New Right in American History.* Chapel Hill: University of North Carolina Press, 1988.

Condon, Peter. "Knownothingism." *The Catholic Encyclopedia.* Vol. 8. New York: Robert Appleton Company, 1910.

Formisano, Ronald P. *For the People: American Populist Movements from the Revolution to the 1850s.* Chapel Hill: University of North Carolina Press, 2008.

Handlin, Oscar. *Boston's Immigrants, 1790–1880: A Study in Acculturation.* Cambridge, MA: Harvard University Press, 1991. First published in 1941.

Jane Toppan

Albright, Evan J. "The First Cape Cod Serial Killer." March 16, 2002. Accessed November 10, 2011. http://capecodconfidential.com/.

Allen, Emily. Alana Averill, and Emmeline Cook. "Jane Toppan, 'Jolly Jane.'" Research paper, Department of Psychology, Radford University, Radford, VA, 2005.

"An Extraordinary Case of Moral Insanity." *New York Times.* October 23, 1904.

Kelleher, Michael and C. L. Kelleher. *Murder Most Rare: The Female Serial Killer.* Westport, CT: Praeger, 1998.

"The Modern Lucretia Borgia Haunted by the Phantoms of Her Victims, Is Facing Death." *Washington Times.* October 21, 1906.

Ramsland, Katherine. "When Women Kill Together." *The Forensic Examiner,* Springfield, MO. Vol. 16. 2007.

Schechter, Harold. *The Serial Killer Files: The Who, What, Where, How and Why of the World's Most Terrifying Murders.* New York: Random House, 2003.

Shattuck, Dr. George. "Is Jane Toppan Responsible?" *Boston Medical and Surgical Journal.* Vol. 147. July 1902.

Wolcott, Martin Gilman. *The Evil 100.* New York: Kensington Publishing, 2002.

Webster Thayer

Dante Alighieri Society of Massachusetts. "Italian-American Heritage." Accessed February 22, 2012. www.dantemass.org/html/italian-american-heritage.html.

Frankfurter, Felix. "The Case of Sacco and Vanzetti." *Atlantic Monthly*. March 1927.

Russell, Francis. *Tragedy in Dedham: The Story of the Sacco-Vanzetti Case*. New York: McGraw-Hill, 1962.

Southwick, Albert B. "Benchley Shocks Worcester." *Worcester Sunday Telegram*. July 5, 2012.

Watson, Bruce. *Sacco & Vanzetti: The Men, the Murders and the Judgment of Mankind*. New York: Viking, 2007.

Yemma, John. "Crimes of the Century: Where Injustice Prevailed, Debate Lingers." *Boston Globe*. November 1, 1999.

J. Franklin Chase

Boyer, Paul S. *Purity in Print: The Vice-Society Movement and Book Censorship in America*. New York: Charles Scribner's Sons, 1968.

Finan, Christopher M. *From the Palmer Raids to the Patriot Act: A History of the Fight for Free Speech in America*. Boston: Beacon Press, 2007.

Kane, Paula M. *Separatism and Subculture: Boston Catholicism, 1900–1920*. Chapel Hill: University of North Carolina Press, 1994.

Miller, Neil. *Banned in Boston: The Ward and Watch Society's Crusade Against Books, Burlesque and the Social Evil*. Boston: Beacon Press, 2010.

Rodgers, Marion Elizabeth. *Mencken: The American Iconoclast*. New York: Oxford University Press, 2005.

Wood, A. L. S. "Keeping the Puritans Pure." *American Mercury*, September 1925.

James Michael Curley

Beatty, Jack. *The Rascal King: The Life and Times of James Michael Curley, 1874–1958*. Reading, MA: Addison-Wesley, 1992.

Connolly, Michael C. "The First Hurrah: James Michael Curley versus the 'Goo-Goos' in the Boston Mayoralty Election of 1914." *Historical Journal of Massachusetts*. Winter 2002.

Curley, James Michael. *I'd Do It Again: A Record of All My Uproarious Years*. Englewood Cliffs, NJ: Prentice-Hall, 1957.

Dinneen, Joseph F. *The Purple Shamrock: The Hon. James Michael Curley of Boston*. New York: W. W. Norton & Co., 1949.

Goodwin, Doris Kearns. *The Fitzgeralds and the Kennedys: An American Saga*. New York: St. Martin's Press, 1991.

Handlin, Oscar. *Boston's Immigrants, 1790–1880: A Study in Acculturation*. Cambridge: Harvard University Press, 1991. First published in 1941.

Luthin, Reinhard H. and Allan Nevins. *American Demagogues: Twentieth Century*. Boston: Beacon Press, 1954.

Trout, Charles. "Curley of Boston: The Search for Irish Legitimacy" Essay. *Boston, 1700–1980: The Evolution of Urban Politics*. Ronald P. Formisano and Constance K. Burns. Westport, CT: Greenwood Press, 1984.

Arthur P. Jell

"Huge Molasses Tank Explodes in North End; 11 Dead, 50 Hurt." *Boston Post*. January 16, 1919.

Lyons, Chuck. "A Sticky Tragedy: The Rupture of a Giant Molasses Tank in Boston Just after the First World War Caused

Devastation and Led to the Longest Legal Case in the City's History." *History Today* (London). January 2009.

Mason, John. "The Molasses Disaster of January 15, 1919." *Yankee Magazine*. January 1965.

Park, Edwards. "Without Warning, Molasses in January Surged over Boston." *Smithsonian*. November 1983.

Puleo, Stephen. *Dark Tide: The Great Boston Molasses Flood of 1919*. Boston: Beacon Press, 2003.

Harry Frazee

Frommer, Harvey. "The 90th Anniversary of Babe Ruth's Major League Debut." Accessed September 13, 2011. www .baseballguru.com.

Johnson, Richard and Glenn Stout. *Red Sox Century: The Definitive History of Baseball's Most Storied Franchise*. New York: Houghton Mifflin, 2005.

Levitt, Dan, Matthew Levitt, and Mark Armour. "Harry Frazee and the Red Sox." The Society for American Baseball Research's *Baseball Research Journal*. No. 37. 2008. Accessed September 15, 2011. http://sabr.org.

Lynch, Michael T. Jr.. *Harry Frazee, Ban Johnson and the Feud That Nearly Destroyed the American League*. Jefferson, NC: McFarland & Co. Publishers, 2008.

Montville, Leigh. *The Big Bam, the Life and Times of Babe Ruth*. New York: Random House Digital, 2007.

Ryan, Bob. "Playing Hit and Miss with the Fabled Curse." *Boston Globe*. January 3, 2001.

Shaughnessy, Dan. "Story Turned into a Bestseller: Sale of Ruth Supported by Frazee's Descendants." *Boston Globe*. September 5, 2003.

Stout, Glenn. "A Curse Born of Hate." 2004. Accessed September 15, 2011. ESPN.com.

Charles Ponzi

Darby, Mary. "In Ponzi We Trust, Borrowing from Peter to Pay Paul Is a Scheme Made Famous by Charles Ponzi. Who Was This Crook Whose Name Graces This Scam?" *Smithsonian.* December 1998.

Dunn, Donald H. *Ponzi! The Boston Swindler.* New York: McGraw-Hill, 1975.

Dunn, Donald H. *Ponzi, The Incredible True Story of the King of Financial Cons.* New York: Broadway Books, 2004.

Ponzi, Charles. *The Rise of Mister Ponzi.* 1920. Reprint, Naples, FL: Inkwell Publishers, 2001.

Train, John. *Famous Financial Fiascos.* London: G. Allen and Unwin, 1985.

Zuckoff, Mitchell. *Ponzi's Scheme: The True Story of a Financial Legend.* New York: Random House, 2005.

Barney Welansky

Benzaquin, Paul. *Holocaust! The Shocking Story of the Boston Cocoanut Grove Fire.* New York: Henry Holt and Company, 1957.

Chertkoff, Jerome M. and Russell H. Kushigian. *Don't Panic: The Psychology of Emergency Egress and Ingress.* Westport, CT: Praeger, 1999.

Esposito, John. *Fire in the Grove, The Cocoanut Grove Tragedy and its Aftermath.* Cambridge, MA: Da Capo Press, 2005.

"Fire Story: The Cocoanut Grove Fire." Boston Fire Historical Society website. Accessed September 20, 2012. www.bostonfirehistory .org/firestory11281942.html.

Schorow, Stephanie. *The Cocoanut Grove Fire*. Beverly, MA: Commonwealth Editions, 2005.

Thomas, Jack. "50 years ago this week, 492 died in a tragedy for the ages." *Boston Globe*. November 22, 1992.

Specs O'Keefe

Behn, Noel. *Big Stick-up at Brink's!* New York: G. P. Putnam's Sons, 1977.

"The Brinks Robbery." The Federal Bureau of Investigation website. Accessed October 10, 2012. www.fbi.gov/about-us/history/famous-cases/brinks-robbery.

Buchanan, William. "Famous Brink's Job Still a Story to Remember." *Boston Globe*. January 17, 1980.

Connolly, Richard. "Specs O'Keefe Is a Free Man but a Prisoner of His Past." *Boston Globe*. January 14, 1975.

Cunningham, Bill. "Brink's Bandetti." *Boston Herald*. January 20, 1950.

O'Keefe, Joseph James "Specs," as told to Bob Considine. *The Men Who Robbed Brink's: One of the Most Famous Holdups in the History of Crime*. New York: Random House, 1961.

Rodriguez, Cindy. "In Low-Tech '50s, Gang Did Unimaginable: Crimes of the Century: Brink's Robbery." *Boston Globe*. October 25, 1999.

Schorow, Stephanie. *The Crime of the Century: How the Brink's Robbers Stole Millions and the Hearts of Boston*. Beverly, MA: Commonwealth Editions, 2008.

Albert DeSalvo

Aronson, Harvey and F. Lee Bailey. *The Defense Never Rests*. New York: Stein Publishing, 1971.

The Biography Channel. "The Boston Strangler." 1987.

Frank, Gerold. *The Boston Strangler.* New York: New American Library, 1966.

Kelly, Susan. *The Boston Stranglers: The Public Conviction of Albert DeSalvo and the True Story of Eleven Shocking Murders.* New York: Kensington Publishing, 2002. First published by Citadel in 1995.

Leyton, Elliot. *Hunting Humans: The Rise of the Modern Multiple Murderer.* New York: Carroll & Graf Publishers, 2003. First published in 1986.

McLaughlin, Loretta. "When Fear Was in Season: Remembering the 30-year-old Boston Strangler Case." *Boston Globe.* June 7, 1992.

Powers, Martine. "Memories of the Strangler: 50 Years Later, People Are Still Fascinated." *Boston Globe.* June 14, 2012.

Thomas, Jack. "In the Grip of Fear: Forty Years Ago This Week, the Boston Strangler Killed His First Victim." *Boston Globe.* June 13, 2002.

Charles M. Stuart

Butterfield, Fox with Constance L. Hays. "A Boston Tragedy: The Stuart Case—A Special Case; Motive Remains a Mystery in Deaths That Haunt a City," *New York Times.* January 15, 1990.

Coontz, Stephanie. *The Way We Never Were: American Families and the Nostalgia Trap.* New York: Basic Books, 1992.

Cullen, Kevin, Sean Murphy, and Mike Barnicle. "Stuart Dies in Jump Off Tobin Bridge After Police Are Told He Killed His Wife." *Boston Globe.* January 5, 1990.

Cullen, Kevin. "Stuart Case Leaves Legacy of Bitterness." *Boston Globe.* October 23, 1994.

Dyson, Michael Eric. *Race Rules: Navigating the Color Line.* Reading, MA: Addison-Wesley, 1996.

Feagin, Joe R. *White Racism: The Basics.* New York: Routledge, 2001.

Guilfoil, John M. "Official Says Stuart Likely Overdosed." *Boston Globe.* September 6, 2011.

Howe, Peter J. and Jerry Thomas. "Reading Woman Dies After Shooting in Car; Husband, Baby Termed Critical." *Boston Globe.* October 25, 1989.

Jacobs, Sally and Anthony Flint. "The Enigma of Charles Stuart." *Boston Globe.* January 28, 1990.

Koch, Tom. *Journalism for the 21st Century: Online Information, Electronic Databases, and the News.* Westport, CT: Praeger, 1991.

Prothrow-Stith, Deborah and Howard R. Spivak. *Murder Is No Accident: Understanding and Preventing Youth Violence in America.* San Francisco: Jossey-Bass, 2004.

Index

Italicized page numbers indicate illustrations.

About the Author

Paul Della Valle, father of three and grandfather of two, lives on five acres of an old farm in Sterling, Massachusetts, with his wife Karen; Yaz, the world's greatest dog; and Boots Vanzetti, their anarchist cat. A golf addict, he mows two of the acres so he can practice hitting full wedges.

Della Valle won dozens of writing and reporting awards in a thirty-year career as a journalist that began even before he graduated from Metropolitan State College in Denver in 1979. In 1996 he founded the *Lancaster Times* and *Clinton Courier,* which he published for nine years. During that time, the combined newspapers were twice runner-up for New England Press Association Newspaper of the Year. He has taught writing at Worcester's Clark University and journalism at Boston's Northeastern University.

He is also a songwriter, and sings and plays guitar with two bands: the Worcester County Bluegrass All Stars and Lizzie O'Dowd and the Sheep Shaggers. In 2009 Globe Pequot Press published his book *Massachusetts Troublemakers: Rebels, Reformers, and Radicals from the Bay State.* Noted *Boston Globe* book critic David Mehegan said of *Massachusetts Troublemakers,* "It's a lively survey of spirited characters . . . It reminds us how much we need people who yank our collective social beards, people who know they are different and are happy to be."

While researching the life of Horace Mann for that book, Della Valle was motivated to become a public schoolteacher. He now joyously teaches English to Clinton High School students who inspire him every day.